Practicing Christians, Practical Atheists

Practicing Christians, Practical Atheists

How Cultural Liturgies and Everyday Social Practices Shape the Christian Life

Phil Davignon

CASCADE *Books* · Eugene, Oregon

PRACTICING CHRISTIANS, PRACTICAL ATHEISTS
How Cultural Liturgies and Everyday Social Practices Shape the Christian Life

Copyright © 2023 Phil Davignon. All rights reserved. Except for brief quotations in critical publications or reviews, no part of this book may be reproduced in any manner without prior written permission from the publisher. Write: Permissions, Wipf and Stock Publishers, 199 W. 8th Ave., Suite 3, Eugene, OR 97401.

Cascade Books
An Imprint of Wipf and Stock Publishers
199 W. 8th Ave., Suite 3
Eugene, OR 97401

www.wipfandstock.com

PAPERBACK ISBN: 978-1-6667-3736-3
HARDCOVER ISBN: 978-1-6667-9670-4
EBOOK ISBN: 978-1-6667-9671-1

Cataloguing-in-Publication data:

Names: Davignon, Phil, author.

Title: Practicing Christians, practical atheists : how cultural liturgies and everyday social practices shape the Christian life / Phil Davignon.

Description: Eugene, OR: Cascade Books, 2023 | Includes bibliographical references and index.

Identifiers: ISBN 978-1-6667-3736-3 (paperback) | ISBN 978-1-6667-9670-4 (hardcover) | ISBN 978-1-6667-9671-1 (ebook)

Subjects: LCSH: Liturgics. | Christianity and culture. | Liturgical adaptation.

Classification: BV178 .D30 2023 (print) | BV178 (ebook)

01/27/23

Contents

List of Tables | vii
Acknowledgments | ix
Introduction | xi

1. Religion, Culture, and Secularization | 1
2. Education | 20
3. Work | 35
4. Consumption | 51
5. Leisure and Rest | 66
6. Counterfeit Virtue and Practical Atheism | 79
7. The Church's Response | 89
8. The True Politics of the Church | 106
9. Epilogue | 122

Bibliography | 125
Index | 139

List of Tables

Table 1: The Eucharist vs. Anti-Eucharistic Consumer Culture | 61

Acknowledgments

WRITING A BOOK IS a long and arduous process and would not have been possible without the encouragement and support of colleagues, friends, and family. Many thanks to Jason Crawford, Jay Beavers, Joy Moore, and Jacob Shatzer for their feedback during our faculty writing group. Your insights and suggestions were invaluable, and I have grown as a writer by observing your approach to writing over the past few years.

I am also thankful for the members of the Jones Suite at Union University, whose intellectual camaraderie has been essential to my formation as a teacher and a scholar. I am especially grateful to Matt Henderson, Justin Barnard, Scott Huelin, Rebecca Edgren, and Nan Thomas for their feedback, support, and example. I would also like to thank Germaine McKenzie, Mike Sauter, and Reuben Dettman for commenting on various drafts throughout this process, and several capable student workers who helped format the bibliography, including Ben Murray, Maggie Wills, Hannah Griffin, and Ethan Judge.

This project was also supported by grants from Pew Research and the Yale Center for Faith and Culture, which encouraged me to develop several of the ideas in this book related to secularization and the formative power of intentional communities. Finally, I am thankful for the ceaseless prayers and support of my parents, Paul and Patrice, and for my wife, Melissa, whose love and encouragement sustains me.

Ad majorem Dei gloriam

Introduction

ONE ENDURING QUESTION FACING Christians—both Catholic and Protestant—is how best to engage with the surrounding culture. Pope Paul VI noted, "The split between the Gospel and culture is without a doubt the drama of our time, just as it was of other times,"[1] while Tim Keller has recently claimed, "There is no more crucial issue facing us today than the relationship of the church and the Gospel to contemporary culture."[2] For Christians the 1960s marked a new era of openness toward mainstream culture, as many fundamentalists who had previously sought purity from the world adopted a more evangelical approach through cultural engagement.[3] Similarly, the Second Vatican Council (1962–1965) famously opened the Catholic Church to the modern world. Being "in the world but not of the world" had become a new rallying cry for Christians.

Yet Christianity's increasing openness toward the world coincided with the turmoil and social change of the 1960s, which led most denominations to experience a widespread loss of religious belief, practice, and adherence.[4] These declines eventually leveled off, as weekly church attendance hovered around 50 percent from the early 1970s to early 1990s,[5]

---

1. Paul VI, *Evangelii Nuntiandi*, sec. 20.
2. Carson, *Christ and Culture Revisited* (back cover).
3. Marsden, *Religion and American Culture*, 242–72.
4. Brown, "Religious Crisis," 468–72.
5. Miller and Nakamura, "Stability of Church Attendance," 276.

Introduction

while church membership held steady at 70 percent.[6] Nevertheless many Christians retained an uneasy relationship with the surrounding world—seeking relevance while maintaining a posture of critique and distinction. How would this posture shape the church's efforts to transmit its essential teachings and practices to future generations?

The tenuous stability of the latter half of the twentieth century eventually gave way to additional declines in the 2000s, as the percentage of Americans who claim no affiliation rose from 10 percent in 2007 to nearly 30 percent in 2021,[7] including 40 percent of millennials.[8] In the United States, for each person who becomes Catholic an average of 6.5 people leave the Church, and over half of those raised Catholic leave the Church at some point in their life.[9] Similarly, the Southern Baptist Convention reported thirteen consecutive years[10] of declining membership, along with a 4 percent decline in baptisms from 2018 to 2019 alone.[11]

Those who continue to identify as Christian and attend church often exhibit low levels of religious practice and theological knowledge. Evangelicals may continue to affirm the importance and authority of Scripture, yet nearly two out of three unwittingly assent to the tenets of Arianism.[12] Among Catholics who have retained their Catholic identity, only about one in four attend Mass on a weekly basis.[13] Many are also ignorant of Catholicism's fundamental teachings, as 49 percent of laypeople erroneously believe the Catholic Church teaches that the bread and wine used during communion are only symbols of the body and blood of Christ. This ignorance was not limited to those who are Catholic in name only, as 24 percent of Catholics who attend Mass weekly also share this mistaken belief.[14]

These alarming trends related to religious adherence, practice, and knowledge have incited a frantic search for the causes and solutions to this growing crisis. Many point to a loss of morality in the public square,[15]

---

6. Jones, "U.S. Church Membership," see table.
7. Smith, "Religiously Unaffiliated," para 3.
8. Pew Research Center, "Decline of Christianity," para. 1.
9. Pew Research Center, "America's Changing Religious Landscape," see table.
10. Before the coronavirus pandemic.
11. Staff reports, "Statistical Decline," para. 21.
12. Lindgren, "State of Theology," para. 7.
13. Center for Applied Research, "Frequently Requested Church Statistics," see table.
14. Data analyzed from D'Antonio et al., "American Catholic Laity Poll, 2011."
15. Neuhaus, *American Babylon*, 1–26.

Introduction

especially in the areas of public education and the media.[16] Others believe the sexual revolution weakened the institution of the family, thereby undermining the faith formation of children.[17] Another camp of critics believes these religious declines have less to do with external social and cultural conditions, and instead blames congregations for failing to adequately form their members by watering down the gospel in a misguided effort to gain members.[18] Many Catholics point to Vatican II as the watershed moment when the Catholic Church relinquished its rich traditions and liturgy in an attempt to appear relevant.[19] Others criticize what they perceive to be collusion with political causes or movements—such as critical race theory or Christian nationalism—while some think the opposite: that the church has undermined its moral integrity by remaining silent on important political issues such as race or sexuality. Still others believe the church became complacent by assuming the next generation would automatically adopt Christian faith in adulthood. Both Catholics and Protestants have turned to innovative approaches to evangelization, church growth, and improving the "weekend experience" in an effort to revive their congregations.[20]

The presence of religion in the public square, the practice of the liturgy, and strategies for evangelization and discipleship are certainly important topics that deserve extended discussion. Yet this book argues that the fundamental challenge of modern age is not defined by these issues. Rather, at the heart of the crisis facing the church is a deeper cultural dysfunction that undermines Christian formation in a myriad of ways most fail to realize.

Christians Engaging Culture

Raymond Williams claimed that the word *culture* is "one of the two or three most complicated words in the English language."[21] This one word is burdened with articulating much depth, nuance, and diversity across various facets of human life. Understanding and appreciating how culture shapes people's lives is certainly essential, but far too often Christians who aspire to engage, change, or "evangelize" the culture rely on a superficial

16. Smith, Ritzet, and Rotolo, *Religious Parenting*, 50–104.
17. Eberstadt, *New Theory of Secularization*, 133–37.
18. Bergler, *Juvenilization of American Christianity*, 1–18.
19. Kwasniewski, *Reclaiming Our Catholic Birthright*, 77–86.
20. White and Corcoran, *Rebuilt*, 93.
21. Williams, *Keywords*, 49.

Introduction

understanding of what it is and how it influences people. The result is that many Christians are quick to adopt a general posture toward culture—either embracing or rejecting it—rather than engaging in a deep assessment of how specific forms of culture shape the Christian life.

One renowned analysis of Christianity and culture is found in H. Richard Niebuhr's *Christ and Culture*, which offers a typology of the postures Christians might take toward their surrounding culture. Niebuhr tells how Christians have historically stood "against" culture, "with" culture, or adopted a variety of middle positions, which Niebuhr identifies as Christ "above", in "paradox" to, or "transforming" culture.[22] Niebuhr's survey of these various postures remains influential—despite numerous critiques and refinements—because it describes how Christians might respond to the inherent tension between Christianity and the world. But how useful is this typology for instructing Christians on living wisely in relation to contemporary forms of culture? While Niebuhr privileges the category of "Christ transforming culture," his approach functionally treats culture as a unified whole.[23] As a result, toward the end of his book he admits that no single approach applies to all circumstances and issues.[24]

In a similar way Vatican II relied on an oversimplified view of culture as it ushered the Catholic Church from a posture of combativeness to openness. The Council has been critiqued for failing to clearly distinguish between modernity as a historical age—which includes many laudable achievements—and modernity as a cultural formation—which rests on various assumptions about the nature of God, creation, and the human person.[25] Upon hearing about the Catholic Church's shift toward accommodation, Karl Barth famously quipped, "Accommodation to what?"[26] Modern culture is not monolithic, meaning Christians cannot answer the question of "Christ and culture" solely by adopting one posture toward the world. Without a more nuanced understanding of culture and cultural influence, Christians risk haphazardly rejecting or embracing various aspects of culture—*either* of which could compromise the church's mission in the modern age. Rather than trying to distill the single best posture toward culture from Scripture and church

---

22. Niebuhr, *Christ and Culture*, 39–44.
23. This is true even though Niebuhr argues culture is not a unified whole.
24. Niebuhr, *Christ and Culture*, 236.
25. Rowland, *Culture and the Thomist Tradition*, 12–14.
26. Rowland, *Culture and the Thomist Tradition*, 19.

Introduction

history, Christians need to discern how specific aspects of culture shape their ability to embody the gospel in the modern age.

The Influence of Cultural Liturgies

One such approach to understanding how culture influences the Christian life is found in James K. A. Smith's groundbreaking work on cultural liturgies.[27] Smith describes how many Christians believe human behavior is primarily driven by beliefs and ideas, which implies that the primary task of the Christian life is to develop the right worldview.[28] Smith's work draws on a host of philosophical, theological, and social scientific sources to argue that this perspective is fundamentally flawed. This is not to say that ideas and worldviews are unimportant (Smith is a philosopher, after all), but to emphasize how human behavior is motivated first and foremost by what people envision as good, which animates their deepest desires. What people desire as ultimate shapes what they worship, which is what truly motivates their daily decisions and life trajectories.

Smith's emphasis on imagination and desire over belief and worldview also unlocks a new understanding of culture and cultural influence. Culture is not just a sea of ideas that determines what people believe, but rather it is embedded within the routines of daily life, and therefore shapes people's hearts in ways they may fail to realize. This deeper form of desire-shaping culture is transmitted primarily through social practices, rather than exposure to ideas. Smith calls these practices "cultural liturgies": embodied experiences that lead into a kind of worship by shaping people's ultimate desires and endowing them with a sense of identity.[29] Two places that offer powerful cultural liturgies are sporting events and shopping malls, which influence what people love not through arguments, but by appealing to their senses in order to capture their hearts.[30] This paradigm-shifting approach to understanding cultural transmission should challenge congregations to question whether their approach to ministry is embodied and liturgical—and thus deeply formative—or rather relies upon an "information delivery" model in an effort to encourage orthodox belief and behavior.

---

27. See especially Smith, *Desiring the Kingdom* and *Imagining the Kingdom*.
28. Smith, *Desiring the Kingdom*, 17–18.
29. Smith, *Desiring the Kingdom*, 80–88.
30. Smith, *Desiring the Kingdom*, 19–25.

Introduction

Plan and Implications of This Book

Smith's theory of cultural liturgies is innovative and insightful, and offers a better approach to understanding cultural influence. But rather than engaging in an extensive analysis of culture, Smith limits his assessment to highly meaningful "thick practices"—cultural liturgies—that overtly shape people's identities in significant ways. Yet people's lives are not only shaped by cultural liturgies such as sporting events and trips to the mall (which are relatively infrequent), but by a whole host of social practices that govern everyday life. Smith acknowledges that everyday ("thin") practices also shape people's desires, stating, "Even our thinnest practices and habits get hooked up into desires that point at something ultimate,"[31] but his analysis of cultural liturgies does not include these everyday social practices.

This book builds upon Smith's work by offering a more comprehensive analysis of how culture influences the Christian life that assesses *both* thin and thick practices. Culture is not only transmitted through liturgies that directly shape people's desires, imagination, and identity, but also within more mundane social practices that quietly form enduring dispositions (virtues or vices). Even if these dispositions do not directly shape one's ultimate desires, they still incline people to think, feel, and act in ways that are either hospitable or inhospitable to the Christian life. C. S. Lewis says, "Every time you make a choice you are turning the central part of you, the part of you that chooses, into something a little different from what it was before. And taking your life as a whole, with all your innumerable choices, all your life long you are slowly turning this central thing either into a heavenly creature or into a hellish creature."[32] How do people's everyday choices, which are often governed by social practices, shape their ability to live faithfully in today's world?

The goal of this book is to offer a comprehensive assessment of how modern forms of culture—embedded in thin (everyday) and thick (cultural liturgies) social practices—influence Christians who are striving to live faithfully in today's age. This task requires both theological and sociological approaches to understanding culture and cultural influence. The tools of sociology allow for a deeper understanding of culture and how it influences people, while theological perspectives are essential for assessing culture's roots in light of the gospel. More specifically, the argument proceeds as follows:

---

31. Smith, *Desiring the Kingdom*, 83.
32. Lewis, *Mere Christianity*, 92.

Introduction

1. *This book grounds its analysis on John Paul II's theological assessment of modern culture, which he criticized as a "culture of death."*

    John Paul II has been called a "theologian of culture" since much of his papal writing assessed the dysfunction of modern forms of culture. This book will engage with his critique of the "culture of death," which enables us to see how culture is more than its surface-level manifestations—whether overtly moral or immoral—but rather it is rooted in underlying assumptions about the nature of the created world, the human person, and what it means to live a good life. These underlying assumptions do not influence people through cultural osmosis, but rather reflect a certain "logic," which shapes people's lives through concrete social practices within everyday life. Chapter 1 will evaluate whether modern culture is conducive to living in light of God's presence and goodness, resulting in a gift of self, or whether it encourages people to be self-centered.

2. *This book employs sociological theories of culture to reveal how culture shapes people's dispositions, behavior, and vision of reality within the social practices of everyday life.*

    Many critics of modernity rely on a superficial understanding of culture, envisioning cultural influence solely as the transmission of overt ideas, norms, and values. Yet sociological models of culture suggest it is most powerfully transmitted through implicit means—within taken-for-granted habits, routines, and practices. Such practices are embedded with culture's underlying form, which become imprinted in people's hearts and minds (more in chapter 1). Chapters 2–5 assess how the culture of death is manifested and transmitted through the seemingly harmless everyday practices related to modern forms of education (chapter 2), work (chapter 3), consumption (chapter 4), and leisure (chapter 5). These domains of life are not independent of each other, but together comprise a deep and pervasive social structure that fosters habits and dispositions that undermine people's ability to fully embody the Christian faith in their everyday lives.

3. *This book provides a clearer vision of how modern society and culture are secularizing.*

    This more robust vision of religion and cultural influence, combined with a theological assessment of culture, allows for a deeper understanding of secularity. Many envision the question of secularization primarily as a matter of numbers—scrutinizing whether rates of

Introduction

church attendance, religious identity, and belief are decreasing. This book argues that the Christian life cannot be reduced to such superficial religiosity. Rather, a more holistic approach to understanding secular cultural influence must account for the ways that modern culture initiates people into habits of mind and heart that undermine their ability to truly embody the Christian faith. Such secular dispositions hinder communion with God and neighbor, even among practicing Christians, and foster what John Paul II and others have called practical atheism—or living as if God does not exist. This is the deepest sense of what it means to be secular and should be the starting point for understanding how modernity challenges the mission of the church.

4. *This book highlights the challenge of discipleship and formation in the modern age.*

This assessment of modern culture and the Christian faith reveals how religiosity and secularity can coexist, both within the church and the lives of its members. Yet the church's response to this catechetical crisis often focuses on halting and reversing the measurable declines in religious belief and activity, which are symptoms of the crisis rather than its underlying cause. Many congregations have become overly reliant on the "ministry-industrial complex": a menu of programs and resources that may inform and inspire their members but is unable to provide the kind of formation necessary to offset the secularizing effects of modern culture (chapter 7). Being a Christian involves more than believing in God and attending church, but coming to embody the dispositions and virtues of the Christian life. What sort of social and cultural infrastructure is needed to sustain such a life? Resisting the deforming influence of the culture of death will require the creation and revival of institutions and practices that offer the kind of daily, embodied formation necessary for life in Christ (chapter 8).[33]

---

33. This book's project shares many similarities with the work of Stanley Hauerwas, who aims to reveal that "salvation is being grafted into practices that save us from those powers that would rule our lives making it impossible for us to truly worship God." *In Good Company*, Introduction.

― 1 ―

Religion, Culture, and Secularization

MANY CHRISTIANS ARE CAPTIVATED by the idea of harnessing culture's power for the sake of the kingdom. Promotional materials for various Christian institutions are rife with phrases such as "changing culture," "engaging culture," "transforming culture," or "evangelizing the culture."[1] Even though culture is a multifaceted concept ("one of the most complicated words in the English language"[2]), people tend to use the word without any sort of qualification. When Christians talk about "the culture," they seem to have in mind a collection of phenomena, trends, and widely shared ideas that are contrary to the Christian faith. When concepts such as consumerism, individualism, and relativism are used to describe what is wrong with the world today, many Christians will nod their heads in agreement, calling to mind examples from media, higher education, and other institutions. Christian parents and leaders can clearly see how these features of culture might be secularizing, and well-meaning cultural critics imagine their task as evaluating such messages and combatting them with Christian messages, whether through sermons, lectures, or Christian media.

While these ways of talking about culture have become quite prevalent, they reveal a misguided understanding of what culture is, how it develops, and how it shapes the Christian life. Referring to "the culture" betrays a subtle assumption that it blankets people with the same effect. If

---

1. See Andy Crouch's *Culture Making* (68–70) for a discussion of various ways Christians engage with culture.
2. Williams, *Keywords*, 49.

pressed, armchair cultural critics might acknowledge that culture's influence is not so uniform, yet the way most people talk about "the culture" subtly reinforces this notion in people's minds. Parents are right to question how culture influences their children's faith, since some form of religion or worship is always at the heart of culture.[3]

Yet many Christians are surprisingly ill-equipped to think about how modern culture influences their faith because they take a narrow view of both culture and religion—understanding culture primarily as overt ideas and values, and religion as beliefs and activities (i.e., church attendance). Of course, culture and religion do include these basic components, but Christians tend to focus on these surface-level phenomena to the exclusion of other more foundational aspects of culture and religion. This chapter offers a more precise understanding of culture and how it is transmitted, which allows for a deeper assessment of how modern forms of culture shape the Christian life.

A Deeper Understanding of Religion, Culture, and Secularization

One of the most crucial issues facing contemporary Christians is whether contemporary forms of culture are secularizing—and how to respond. The word *secular* comes from the root *saeculum*, meaning "of the age." Many Christian leaders are quick to denounce the worldliness of contemporary culture—supplementing their critique with various sociological, philosophical, and historical accounts of the secular and secularization. While there is much to learn from these academic perspectives, they often rely on relatively superficial or generic definitions of religion, which limits their ability to inform the church's thinking about the challenge of secularity in today's world. Nevertheless, such academic perspectives remain a helpful starting point for understanding how social, historical, and philosophical developments relate to the church's mission in the contemporary world.

Sociological theories of secularization illustrate how various features of modernity might challenge the Christian faith. One such feature of modernity is *differentiation*, which highlights how religion has become understood as its own domain separate from government, economy, and education. Differentiation is often accompanied by *rationalization*,

---

3. Christopher Dawson's work emphasizes the relationship between religion and culture. See Woods, "Religion," para. 3.

whereby social life becomes governed primarily by instrumental ends rather than religious norms and values. Both differentiation and rationalization lay the groundwork for an autonomous social sphere that operates independently of religious principles.[4] Differentiation and rationalization foster *pluralism* and the *privatization* of religion. When no single religious worldview dominates society, people must choose whether and how to be religious, resulting in an explosion of religious diversity.[5] This growing pluralism makes religious consensus impossible, which reinforces the need to separate religion from public life. This encourages people to privatize their religious beliefs, which become seen as a possible threat to peaceful social order.[6] Even religions themselves face pressure to become increasingly generic by syncretizing with other aspects of culture and becoming a kind of civil religion, or by fulfilling the therapeutic function of helping people to feel good about their lives.[7]

Much of the sociological research on secularization assesses how these four features of modernity (differentiation, rationalization, pluralism, privatization) lead to religious decline. As religion loses its dominance—and eventually its relevance—the world becomes envisioned as disenchanted, or void of supernatural beings and forces.[8] Those who remain religious are confronted by the fact that others do not share their vision of reality—undermining what sociologist Peter Berger called the "plausibility structures" of religious belief.[9] For these reasons, early theorists of secularization overwhelmingly believed that religion was on a course toward extinction. In 1968 Berger (himself a Christian) famously predicted in *The New York Times*, "By the 21st century, religious believers are likely to be found only in small sects, huddled together to resist a worldwide secular culture."[10]

Yet widespread secularization never arrived. While Europe experienced much decline, the United States maintained stable levels of belief in God and church attendance into the year 2000.[11] New theories rooted in an

4. Tschannen, "Secularization Paradigm," 397.

5. Stark and Finke, *Acts of Faith*, 197–99.

6. Cavanaugh, *Theopolitical Imagination*, 6.

7. Rieff, *Triumph of the Therapeutic*, 14–15; Rieff, *Fellow Teachers*, 120. Phillip Rieff pioneered the notion of therapeutic culture.

8. This apparent disenchantment is accompanied by other forms of "enchantment," such as consumerism and nationalism. People's lives can never be truly "disenchanted."

9. Berger, *Sacred Canopy*, 45.

10. "A Bleak Outlook."

11. Stark and Finke, *Acts of Faith*, 61–63.

economic understanding of human behavior argued that religious demand is constant, and individual religiosity will only flourish in free and open religious markets that allow religious entrepreneurs to provide a diverse supply of religious "products" to meet people's varied preferences.[12] Since the United States does not regulate religion or privilege any specific denomination, the market for religion is flooded with a variety of producers who are competing to offer the best religious "products," which induces maximal religious participation. Europe, on other hand, experienced religious declines because many of its governments offered subsidies to national churches, which reduced incentives to innovate, restricted competition, and caused the market for religion to become monolithic.[13]

Not only did the United States avoid widespread secularization, but religion remained strong across the modernizing world: Pentecostalism was booming in the global South and the Middle East witnessed a resurgence in Islamic fundamentalism.[14] As evidence mounted against the original secularization hypothesis, Peter Berger recanted his earlier position, stating, "The world today, with some exceptions . . . is as furiously religious as it ever was, and in some places more so than ever."[15] Perhaps Europe was the exception, not the rule, in regards to religion's fate in the modern age.[16] The relative persistence of religion has led sociologists to largely abandon the project of constructing a general theory of secularization,[17] as modernity and secularization are too nuanced and contingent to be captured in one general theory.[18] Instead of anticipating the demise of religion, the field has shifted its focus to historical case studies, exploring cross-cultural differences, the sacralization of other aspects of social life,[19] and describing other ways religion is changing in the contemporary world.[20]

Religion may not be disappearing, but its expression has taken new forms in today's world. One in three conservative Protestant teens say it is okay to pick and choose one's religious beliefs, rather than assenting to

---

12. Stark and Finke, *Acts of Faith*, 201.
13. Stark and Finke, *Acts of Faith*, 228–39.
14. Gorski and Altinordu, "After Secularization?," 56.
15. Berger, "Secularism in Retreat."
16. Berger, Davie, and Fokas, *Religious America*, 9–22.
17. Some notable exceptions include David Martin and Steve Bruce.
18. Smith and Vaidyanathan, "Multiple Modernities," 250–57.
19. For examples, see Tara Isabella Burton's *Strange Rites*, 1–14.
20. Gorski and Altinordu, "After Secularization?," 75–76.

Religion, Culture, and Secularization

the doctrines of a single religion.[21] A growing number of young people subscribe to what Christian Smith termed moralistic therapeutic deism, viewing God as a sort of divine butler or cosmic therapist to be called upon when needed.[22] Young adults are often content to put faith on the shelf for a few years, retrieving it once they settle down later in life.[23] Nearly 30 percent of Americans now claim "no religion,"[24] as religion is just one of many sources of meaning, purpose, and identity in modern life. Many of these religious "nones" continue to believe in God and practice spirituality from time to time,[25] but they remain untethered from traditional religious institutions.

Contemporary religious expression is rife with such paradoxes and contradictions. The number of Catholics in America has held steady since the year 2000 (due largely to immigration),[26] yet for every person who joins the Catholic Church nearly seven leave.[27] The rate of church attendance among Christians has remained relatively stable from 2009 to 2019, but the percentage of Americans who identify as Christian has declined 12 percent over the same time period.[28] Evangelicals continue to affirm the importance and authority of Scripture, yet nearly two out of three unwittingly express support for the tenets of the Arian heresy.[29] These paradoxical statistics imply the vitality of religion in the twenty-first century cannot be captured simply through superficial religious metrics related to beliefs and activities.

The disciplines of history, philosophy, and theology also explore the effects of rationalization, differentiation, and pluralism, offering rich narratives that trace the genealogy of the secular. Perhaps the most renowned genealogical account of secularization is found in Charles Taylor's *A Secular Age*, which tells a complex story of how all modern people—including Christians—have come to imagine reality on secular terms. Taylor rejects the idea that the growing emphasis on science and reason beginning in the sixteenth and seventeenth centuries simply replaced religion (what Taylor

---

21. Smith and Denton, *Soul Searching*, 77.
22. Smith and Denton, *Soul Searching*, 162–63.
23. Stolzenberg et al., "Religious Participation," 84–103.
24. Smith, "Religiously Unaffiliated," para. 3.
25. Lipka, "Becoming More Secular," see graph.
26. Center for Applied Research, "Frequently Requested Church Statistics," see table.
27. Pew Research Center, "America's Changing Religious Landscape," see table.
28. Pew Research Center, "Decline of Christianity Continues," para. 1.
29. Lindgren, "State of Theology," para. 7.

calls subtraction theories). Rather, his work describes the emergence of a new "modern moral order"[30] that allowed people to conceive of human flourishing apart from God, what Taylor calls "exclusive humanism." Even though many people retained Christian belief and practice, the social order was now firmly grounded in an "immanent frame" rather than a pervasive sense of transcendent reality.

Taylor's narrative offers an innovative way to understand secularization. While he acknowledges definitions of secularization based on differentiation and declines in belief and practice, Taylor proposes a new understanding of secularization based on the "conditions of belief." In pre-modern life people were unable to imagine the world apart from the supernatural, but today people must *choose* to believe in God (or gods) while facing the possibility that the claims of their religion are not true. In other words, people's social imaginaries—how they envision the world and their lives—are no longer inevitably religious.[31] According to Taylor, no one can escape this secular social imaginary. Even pious Christians have lost the ability to imagine the world as an inherently spiritual realm—and instead must strain to envision God's presence in the world while continually being confronted by modern norms and assumptions that paint their religious belief as untrue or irrelevant. People whose lives are disconnected ("buffered") from the spiritual realm will still experience moments of transcendence from time to time, but according to Taylor they can never fully recover an enchanted vision of reality.

Generic Religion vs. Religion as a Virtue

Sociological and genealogical accounts of secularization offer some important insights on the interplay between religion and modernity, but they tend to rely on a generic understanding of religion and remain limited in their ability to help the church understand the challenge of modern secularity. Creating an ideal type ("religion") may be necessary for large-scale analyses of concepts such as religion, democracy, or capitalism. But relying on an ideal type when studying religion inevitably obscures important distinctions

---

30. Due to nominalism and the disenchantment of time and the material world.

31. Taylor generally agrees with Max Weber's notion of disenchantment, but argues that disenchantment is not just a feature of the world, but also people's minds. In other words, meaning itself is no longer objective quality of the world, but is created by individual minds. See Smith, *How (Not) to Be Secular*, 28–29.

and nuances related to various beliefs and practices, the social organization of religion (congregations, denominations), God's presence and action in the world (theodicy), sin, and virtue. These elements are not interchangeable, but are the defining features of specific religions. There is also no such thing as generic religion in lived experience, yet researchers often reduce the complexity and nuance of specific religions for the sake of analysis.

Charles Taylor acknowledges that the question of secularization depends on how we define religion,[32] yet this is no easy task. Ultimately, scholars must choose a definition of religion based on the purpose of their study.[33] Jonathan Z. Smith claims, "'Religion' is not a native term; it is a term created by scholars for their intellectual purposes and therefore is theirs to define."[34] When scholars construct a generic definition of religion they do so for the purpose of conducting the kind of research that is accepted within their fields, which for social scientists involves defining religion in quantifiable terms. While this allows researchers to search for statistical relationships between religion and modernity,[35] it fails to adequately describe the tension between some modern forms of culture and the Christian faith.

Christians in the United States also seem to imagine secularization primarily as a sociological problem: as a decline (or possible decline) in religious beliefs, identity, and church attendance, as made evident by the popularity of studies from faith-based polling groups such as Barna and Lifeway Research.[36] Many Christian leaders seem to imagine the vitality of the church in terms of beliefs and activities—that the Christian life is a matter of holding the right theology, attending church, being active in church ministries, and sharing the good news with others. While these are important components of Christianity, they do not define the Christian life itself.

Charles Taylor's *A Secular Age* takes important step in adopting a more specific understanding of religion by emphasizing that it aims to transform people for a kind of human flourishing that extends beyond this world.[37] This improves upon relatively static definitions (i.e., beliefs and church attendance) by acknowledging that lived religion involves movement toward

---

32. Taylor, *Secular Age*, 429.
33. Schilbrack, "What Isn't Religion?," 292.
34. Smith, "Religion, Religions, Religious," 281.
35. Which fits with the preconceived notions of many social scientists that religion is merely epiphenomenal of other social processes.
36. Wuthnow, "In Polling We Trust," 42.
37. Taylor, *Secular Age*, 427–31.

some end. Taylor focuses on the connection between "conditions of belief" and the possibility of otherworldly transformation: how do people envision transformation toward otherworldly ends in an age governed by immanence? Though this conception of religion is conducive for Taylor's analysis, his description of otherworldly transformation as that "which takes [people] beyond or outside of whatever is normally understood as human flourishing"[38] remains vague. At a high level this describes many religions, but by neglecting to specify the end toward which people are being transformed, Taylor's approach is unable to *fully* explain what it means to be "worldly"—or secular—from a Christian perspective.

Taylor's diagnosis of modern secularity also remains limited because he prioritizes the role of ideas[39] by emphasizing the fact that people cannot attain religious certainty when they live within an "immanent frame." From Taylor's perspective, the modern age is inherently secular because even those who do not actively doubt are unable to attain religious certainty. But from a Christian perspective a lack of certainty (or even the presence of doubt) is not as debilitating as Taylor implies. Peter and Thomas (in)famously doubted Jesus at times, and the apostles are described as doubting prior to Christ's ascension (Matt 28:17). The prayer, "I believe; help my unbelief!" (Mark 9:24) also implies that a lack of certainty and faith are not totally incompatible.

Statistics related to religious decline and the secular social imaginary shed light on some of the challenges facing Christians in the modern age. But each of these modes of understanding secularization rely on notions of religion that are poor approximations of Christianity. The Christian faith is more than maintaining beliefs, attending church, or generic transformation, despite a lack of certainty. Rather, at the heart of the Christian life is what Scripture refers to as *metanoia*—the grace-empowered transformation and renewal of one's mind and heart by turning away from sin.[40] This perspective is consistent with Aquinas and Augustine's understanding of religion (*religio*), which they viewed as more than a system of beliefs, "interior impulse," or institution. Nor would they have limited religion to a supernatural realm separate from worldly activity.[41] Rather, Aquinas argued

---

38. Taylor, *Secular Age*, 430.

39. Though he also acknowledges the importance of practices.

40. Jesus' first words in the Gospel of Mark are a call to metanoia: "The time is fulfilled, and the kingdom of God is at hand; repent, and believe in the Gospel" (Mark 1:15).

41. Cavanaugh, *Myth of Religious Violence*, 65–67.

that religion is best understood as virtue—a set of dispositions that enable people to achieve some good end, which for Christians is conforming their lives to God's will and sanctification. The virtue of religion is made possible by an infusion of God's grace and love, which allows people to devote their lives to God, as well as to surrender their minds to God through prayer.[42] Aquinas and Augustine distinguished between false religion and true religion, which involves habits of prayer and devotion that foster cardinal and theological virtues.[43]

Treating religion as a virtue allows for a more precise understanding of the nature of the Christian life, one where religious beliefs and activities contribute to people's transformation but are not treated merely as ends in themselves. Therefore, the Christian life involves growing in enduring dispositions[44] (*habitus*) that reflect putting on the love of Christ (Col 3:14). External forms of religiosity may be the means through which people receive grace and grow in virtue, but these must be understood in light of their ultimate purpose, which is conversion and transformation.[45] Bad theology and religious inactivity certainly impair the Christian life, and congregations should continue their focus on these aspects of the faith, yet holding the right beliefs and being active in one's congregation is no guarantee of spiritual maturity.

Highlighting this distinction between religion as beliefs and activities—as opposed to religion as a virtue—may seem unnecessary, yet it is essential for understanding how culture shapes people's ability to fully embody the Christian life. Many congregations and ministries either treat religious activity as an end in itself, or overintellectualize faith by conflating theological knowledge with spiritual formation.[46] But if Christian maturity is primarily about God's grace transforming the soul through the cultivation of various dispositions and virtues, then the church must pay far more

---

42. Hütter, "Virtue of Religion," 49. Hütter is summarizing *Summa Theologica*, II-II, q. 83, a. 1.

43. Hütter, "Virtue of Religion," 57–58.

44. Aquinas uses the word *habitus* to describe the internalized, enduring dispositions that shape future action. Habitus cannot be neatly translated as either habit or disposition since it entails more than repeated acts or an inclination to act in a certain way. Rather than using the technical term *habitus*, I will refer to "dispositions" or "enduring dispositions" throughout this book. For a detailed discussion of the difference between habits and dispositions see Miner, "Aquinas on Habitus," 68–72.

45. As Aquinas notes, the internal acts of religion take precedence over the external.

46. Smith, *Desiring the Kingdom*, 40–46.

attention to how modern culture shapes people's underlying dispositions, and not just their stated beliefs and religious activity.

Treating religion as a virtue also helps to contextualize the role of the secular social imaginary. The assumption that the presence of doubt cripples religious transformation relies on an understanding of religion that gives too much weight to ideas and not enough to practices, dispositions, and virtues. Lack of certainty only becomes debilitating when it manifests itself in practices that undermine the virtue of religion and distance people from God. Even people who are certain of their religious beliefs may participate in "cultural liturgies" and practices that undermine the virtue of religion ("This people honors me with their lips, but their heart is far from me" [Matt 15:8]), while others who lack certainty may be enmeshed in communities of faith and engage in practices that work to "make God real."[47]

Of course, it would be a false dichotomy to pit beliefs against practices. Taylor acknowledges that ideas and practices cannot be fully separated,[48] yet his analysis of secularization is centered on the former.[49] Beliefs, certainty, and social imaginaries are certainly important for understanding modern secularity, but at most they are only half of the story. Charles Taylor's *A Secular Age* offers a brilliant genealogy of the development of the secular, but by privileging the role of ideas over practices his analysis is unable to account for the ways that the virtue of religion is shaped by the social practices that govern everyday life. Taylor's analysis is helpful for identifying the presence of the secular social imaginary, but a deeper account must treat secularity as a deficiency in the virtue of religion. This calls for devoting increased attention to practices as the primary determinant of people's enduring dispositions, which not only includes the secular social imaginary, but a host of dispositions of mind and heart. From this perspective, the fact that Christians live under the shadow of a secular social imaginary does not necessarily mean they will be unable to grow in the virtues and dispositions of the Christian faith,[50] which ultimately take precedence over religious certainty.

---

47. Luhrmann, *How God Becomes Real*, xii.
48. Taylor, *Modern Social Imaginaries*, 26.
49. This may be due to the fact that Taylor was influenced by Hegel.
50. The secular social imaginary may operate on a global level, but it is always mediated through the practices and relationships at the local level.

Religion, Culture, and Secularization

How Culture Influences the Virtue of Religion

This deeper understanding of religion as a virtue enables a clearer picture of how modern culture influences the Christian faith. From this perspective, Christians should not only be concerned with the ways culture influences people's beliefs, activities, or social imaginary, but must attend to how culture shapes the necessary virtues and dispositions of the Christian life. Recent sociological theorizing on culture helps to shed light on how culture influences people's dispositions by distinguishing between its explicit and implicit forms.[51] When most Christians think about culture they imagine it in explicit forms, which includes messaging, ideas, and cultural artifacts that are readily apparent. But the form of culture is also implicit—embedded within institutions and social practices. Institutions such as the economy, family, and religion reflect *some* underlying logic that determines how they are organized. This logic informs how people ought to act within these various institutions, endowing them with a sense of identity and meaning.[52]

These implicit forms of culture may seem to have relatively little influence on people's behavior because they remain hidden from sight. But this is not the case. Implicit forms of culture are likely to have a more enduring effect on human behavior because they shape people's underlying dispositions without their conscious consent. Explicit forms of culture may shape people's beliefs and how they talk about their decisions, but they typically have a less enduring influence on people's behavior.[53] The reason is that explicit forms of culture are often transitory: someone may watch a movie that overtly contradicts the Christian faith, while later attending church or theology class. The content of these messages does not infiltrate the minds of people who automatically internalize whatever they hear. Such messaging is relatively uninfluential on its own, but becomes powerful when it is reinforced by/within more enduring relationships, rituals, and ways of life. Explicit culture is only the tip of the iceberg. Culture is most influential when it operates beneath the surface—as implicit culture—slowly and persistently shaping people's habits of mind and heart.

The relative importance of implicit culture is obscured because people easily call to mind explicit forms of culture while remaining unable to articulate implicit forms of culture, which often operate in the background

---

51. Lizardo, "Improving Cultural Analysis," 91–93.
52. Thorton and Ocasio, "Institutional Logics," 804.
53. Lizardo, "Improving Cultural Analysis," 92.

—shaping people's lives in ways they fail to realize. This is consistent with philosopher Michael Polanyi's observation that people "know more than they can tell," and also "tell more than they know how."[54] In other words, people may justify their decisions and behaviors on the basis of beliefs and values that actually have relatively little influence in their life, while being unable to articulate the deeply internalized values and dispositions that truly motivate their behavior and shape their vision of reality.

This does not mean people's stated intentions are unimportant, or that they are unable to act based on deeply held convictions. As rational beings people can and do choose to act on the basis of preexisting commitments and intentions. Yet empirical research suggests the connection between what people say and do is often relatively weak.[55] People almost always explain their behavior using rational justifications, but people are unlikely to deliberate over each and every decision. Instead, they rely upon cognitive shortcuts in the form of schemas, habits, or dispositions.[56] This model of human cognition is supported by recent developments in cognitive psychology and theological models of human action. Cognitive psychology suggests people's behavior is often motivated by deeply internalized dispositions that people are often unable to articulate.[57] Similarly, Aquinas describes how virtues of both the intellect and will are formed through action.[58] Discursive thoughts and intentions can override enduring dispositions, but in general people's actions are driven more by what they love than by what they think.[59]

Of course, explicit and implicit forms of culture are always deeply interconnected. Christian liturgies include explicit elements such as the reading of Scripture, sermons, and the content of the prayers, which cannot be separated from the tacit, embodied aspects of the liturgy: its pace, visual cues, moments of silence, "smells and bells," standing, kneeling, the temperament of ministers and other congregants, and participation in the Eucharist or Lord's Supper. The explicit and implicit aspects of Christian liturgy work in tandem to shape people's spirituality, but arguably the implicit

---

54. This is a summary of Polanyi's position. See Lizardo's "Improving Cultural Analysis," 99.

55. Swidler, *Talk of Love*, 107.

56. Vaisey, "Socrates, Skinner, and Aristotle," 607–8.

57. Wilson, *Strangers to Ourselves*, 4.

58. Aquinas, *Summa Theologica*, I-II, q. 63, a. 2.

59. Smith, *Desiring the Kingdom*, 64.

features mark their imagination long after the content from various messaging fades away.[60] Overt messaging is essential, but on its own will fail to provide deep formation unless accompanied by institutions (e.g., the family, school, and congregation) and embodied practices (e.g., prayer, service, ritual) that shape people's hearts and minds over the long term.[61]

Christian liturgies affirm that the life of faith is far more than mere beliefs and activities, but must be understood as cultivating the kinds of virtues that truly foster life in Christ. Instead of prioritizing how culture influences what people believe, Christians should devote more attention to the ways culture shapes what people love, desire, and envision as good. Both sociological and philosophical theories of action suggest this requires emphasizing the role of practices.[62] This is not to say that ideas and messaging are unimportant, but that Christians must attend to the ways habits and routines work to slowly form them in enduring beliefs, values, and dispositions. James K. A. Smith argues that culture is most formative when embedded within the kinds of rituals, practices, and "liturgies" one might experience at a sporting event or the mall. Such cultural liturgies do not form people by delivering information, but by inviting them into embodied experiences and practices.[63] Many Christians are keenly aware when the content of overt messaging contradicts their faith, but few sense how implicit forms of culture, embedded in various social institutions, cultural

---

60. The sociologist Andrew Greeley argues in *Catholic Imagination* (183–88) that Catholics have a distinctive imagination or sensibility that extends beyond mere belief.

61. The strength of habituated culture over culture that has been internalized and acted upon deliberatively is obscured by the fact that when asked to account for their behavior on a survey or during an interview people are unable (or unaware) to describe the underlying habits and dispositions that shape their behavior. Instead, sociological research suggests that people are quick to draw upon declarative modes of culture when giving oral justification for their beliefs or behavior—even if their behavior is inconsistent with their justifications. See Vaisey, "Motivation and Justification," 1676–82.

62. This usage of practices is broader than Alasdair MacIntyre's definition, which emphasizes the internal goods of human activity that are achieved when people pursue excellence. MacIntyre defines practices as "any coherent and complex form of socially established cooperative human activity through which goods internal to that activity are realized in the course of trying to achieve those standards of excellence which are appropriate to, and partially definitive of, that form of activity, with the result that human powers to achieve excellence, and human conception of the goods involved, are systematically extended." See *After Virtue*, 187. A broader sociological approach is Schatzki's definition of practices as "an open-ended, spatially-temporally dispersed nexus of doings and sayings." Schatzki, "Primer on Practices," 14.

63. Smith, *Desiring the Kingdom*, 93–103.

liturgies, and everyday social practices, can undermine the virtue of religion. How do the defining features of modern life shape people's ability to develop the necessary dispositions and virtues of the Christian life?

The Culture of Death and Practical Atheism

This vision of religion, culture, and secularization requires a new approach to assessing whether contemporary forms of culture are compatible with the Christian life. It is relatively easy to detect when explicit messaging contradicts the Christian faith, yet this mode of cultural transmission is generally less influential compared to forms of culture that are transmitted through everyday practices. Everyday practices seem relatively benign—perhaps leading some to think that they have little influence on the Christian life. But even seemingly neutral institutions and practices are embedded with an underlying logic that reflects *some* answer to questions such as "What is a person?," "What does it mean to live well?," and "What is true freedom?" A deeper evaluation of these underlying logics is essential to understand how modern culture influences the virtues and dispositions that are necessary for growth in the Christian life. Are these logics compatible with a Christian vision of reality? How do they shape our experience of the world, ourselves, and other people? Do the dispositions and habits they foster enable or constrain our pursuit of true human flourishing, understood as communion with God?

Theologian David L. Schindler offers a means of assessing modern culture from a christological perspective. Schindler's approach is founded on the idea that the incarnation reveals the meaning and purpose not only of human life, but of all of creation.[64] Creation will be redeemed by coming to participate in the life of the Trinity, whose form is revealed in the person of Jesus Christ, who is the image of love itself.[65] This love is not merely abstract, disembodied, or emotional, but finds its perfect image in Christ's death, in which Christians are invited to share (Rom 6:3–5). Thus Christian transformation is more than generic self-improvement but

---

64. Schindler warns Christians against the "'accidentalizing' of the historical reality of Jesus Christ: conceiving the event of Jesus Christ as a merely "positive" historical fact rather than as the utterly gratuitous event that (nonetheless) gives nature and history their deepest—indeed, original—meaning and order." Schindler, "Order of Intelligence," 421.

65. Schindler, "Eucharistic Evangelization," 550–551.

allows Christians to embody the form of Christ's self-giving love and make it increasingly present in the world.

Christ's self-giving love not only transforms people's individual lives, but all of the created order, including the human creations of culture and institutions. Even though society will inevitably reflect humanity's fallen nature, Christians must not abandon institutions and culture, but work (through God's grace) to reform them—thereby extending God's love into every area of human existence. Schindler claims that God's love is the most fundamental aspect of reality,[66] which has essential implications for the ordering of human life and society. The Christian life is a response to God's love: humbly and gratefully receiving his gifts—returning them to him as an act of worship. All of creation is sacramental, offering people the opportunity to receive God's grace and love and worship him in return. By receiving God's gifts and returning them to him in love and thanksgiving, Christians are transformed and become the body of Christ. As Augustine heard God saying to him, "You shall feed upon me. And you will not, as with the food of the body, change me into yourself, but you will be changed into me."[67]

This sacramental nature of reality touches every area of life, including society and culture. Institutions such as the family, economy, and education system shape how people inhabit the world, meaning they should be considered in light of humanity's highest calling to holiness and self-sacrificial love. According to Schindler, the goal of life is "to see all of reality as made in the image of the trinitarian God revealed in Jesus Christ, hence the image of the Logos who is (eucharistic) love; that we thereby help to draw out of creation, out of every last fiber of every being in the cosmos, its meaning or order as a creature destined, in and through this love, to glorify the Father."[68]

Despite these lofty intentions, social institutions and their accompanying practices are often rooted in an underlying cultural form that separates people from the deepest truths of reality and hinders communion with God. The modern social order seems to be religiously neutral: since science cannot demonstrate the existence or relevance of any god, public life must not be based on any religious foundation. To some this may seem like a good compromise. Carving out a neutral space where people can live untethered from any religious influence appears to be the only path to peace and unity in a pluralistic society. Of course, religious people may

---

66. Schindler, *Ordering Love*, 1.
67. Augustine, *Confessions*, 7.10.16.
68. Schindler, *Heart of the World*, 168–69.

have their own private beliefs and devotions, but these must remain compartmentalized from public life.

Even though this arrangement may seem neutral, it ends up privileging its own set of assumptions about the nature of the world, human life, and freedom. These assumptions are not religiously neutral, but are best described as agnostic: that God's existence is unknowable through public reason and therefore irrelevant for public life. When God is pushed to the margins, the desires and autonomy of individuals become the basis of social order. This does not produce a society that is religiously neutral, but one that promotes a vision of human life that is often at odds with a Christian vision of goodness.[69]

This underlying foundation of modern society inevitably produces what John Paul II criticized as a "culture of death."[70] John Paul II has been referred to as a "theologian of culture,"[71] since several of his papal encyclicals explored the dysfunctions within modern culture. His critique of the culture of death is insightful because it is theologically rigorous, while going beneath the surface-level content of culture to assess its underlying form. John Paul II introduced the concept of the "culture of death" in his 1995 encyclical *Evangelium Vitae*, which is best known for criticizing the growing acceptance of abortion and euthanasia, yet this encyclical not only condemns these practices but also criticizes the cultural foundation that allowed these practices to arise in the first place. John Paul II refers to the evils of abortion and euthanasia as a "problem which exists at the cultural, social, and political level," and must "be understood not only in terms of the phenomena of death which characterize it but also in the variety of causes which determine it."[72]

For John Paul II the effects of sin extend beyond the individual level. Even though all sin originates in personal decisions, it becomes embedded within social structures and thereby can "grow stronger, spread, and become the source of other sins, and so influence people's behavior."[73] From this perspective sin is not merely interior, but has an "external dimension, which takes its concrete form as the content of culture and civilization, as a

---

69. These differing visions of the good cannot peacefully coexist, unless Christianity becomes a set of private beliefs and devotions with little to no bearing on public life.

70. David Schindler makes this connection in "Order of Intelligence," 419.

71. Dulles, "Theologian of Culture."

72. John Paul II, *Evangelium Vitae*, sec. 18.

73. John Paul II, *Sollicitudo Rei Socialis*, sec. 36.

philosophical system, an ideology, a program for action and for the shaping of human behavior."[74] John Paul II notes that accounting for sin's structural dimension is essential for understanding the place of the church in the modern world, stating "one cannot easily gain a profound understanding of the reality that confronts us unless we give a name to the root of the evils which afflict us."[75]

He identifies the root of the culture of death as a *"loss of contact with God's wise design."*[76] When people are no longer able to perceive God's presence in the world, creation, and their own lives, they lose the ability to see themselves as "'mysteriously different' from other earthly creatures."[77] Similarly, "nature itself, from being 'mater' (mother), is now reduced to being 'matter,' and is subjected to every kind of manipulation."[78] Losing sight of God's wise design results in *"the eclipse of the sense of God."*[79] John Paul II claims this eclipse of the sense of God is "the deepest [root] of the struggle between the 'culture of life' and the 'culture of death,'" which characterizes "a social and cultural climate dominated by secularism."[80] When people lose their sense of God they begin *"living as if God did not exist,"*[81] as their "'quality of life' is interpreted primarily or exclusively as economic efficiency, inordinate consumerism, physical beauty and pleasure, to the neglect of the more profound dimensions—interpersonal, spiritual and religious—of existence."[82] If people lose sight of their higher spiritual purpose as made in the image of God, they begin to imagine themselves as animals whose body is primarily a vehicle for pleasure, and others "not for what they 'are', but for what they 'have, do and produce.'"[83]

It is not difficult to see how God's presence has been eclipsed in popular media, education, and the public square. Contemporary life is full of

---

74. John Paul II, *Dominum Et Vivificantem*, 56. Acknowledging the structural dimension of sin does not negate personal responsibility since only individual people can commit sins. But this concept does reveal how individual sins metastasize, creating social and cultural forms that nudge people toward vice and idolatry.

75. John Paul II, *Sollicitudo Rei Socialis*, sec. 36.

76. John Paul II, *Evangelium Vitae*, sec. 22.

77. John Paul II, *Evangelium Vitae*, sec. 22.

78. John Paul II, *Evangelium Vitae*, sec. 22.

79. John Paul II, *Evangelium Vitae*, sec. 21.

80. John Paul II, *Evangelium Vitae*, sec. 22.

81. John Paul II, *Evangelium Vitae*, sec. 22.

82. John Paul II, *Evangelium Vitae*, sec. 23.

83. John Paul II, *Evangelium Vitae*, sec. 23.

examples of how people, including Christians, have lost sight of God's wise design in creation, in other people, and even in their own bodies. The prevalence of pornography and substance abuse indicate an inordinate focus on pleasure, and contemporary life is full of status symbols indicating what we "have, do, and produce."[84] Since it is so easy to recognize the effects of the culture of death within larger society, Christians might be tempted to write off John Paul II's critique by imagining that it only applies to other people, while they themselves remain relatively immune from its effects.

But such a simplistic dismissal of the culture of death would be mistaken. John Paul II connects the culture of death to the "eclipse of the sense of God," and not necessarily a loss of belief in God's existence. This subtle distinction is important because it implies that even people who believe in God might begin to lose their sense of him. Without a sense of God's presence, Christians may begin living as if God does not exist, even if they generally abide by Christian morality. This is practical atheism. John Paul II warns that the culture of death, with "its ubiquitous tentacles, succeeds at times in putting Christian communities themselves to the test."[85] Christians should not exonerate themselves because they reject the sinful *content* of modern society, but rather must assess how the *form* of modern culture takes shape within the institutions, practices, and routines of everyday life in the modern world.

The Secularity of Modern Culture

This assessment of the modern culture provides a new foundation for assessing the secularity of the contemporary world. Modern secularity is not primarily a matter of overt messaging (i.e., media, education) that contradicts Christianity, but rather it is found within the institutions and practices that govern everyday life, which initiate Christians into a way of life that effectively denies the truth that Christ's love is the basis of reality. For this reason, modern secularity is not manifested primarily in declines in religious belief, identity, and church attendance. At a deeper level, secular culture forms Christians who—despite their religious beliefs, practices, and good intentions—begin to embody secular dispositions of mind and heart.

For this reason, the most serious threat to Christianity in the modern age is not overt atheism, but practical atheism: Christians living as if God

84. John Paul II, *Evangelium Vitae*, sec. 23.
85. John Paul II, *Evangelium Vitae*, sec. 21.

does not exist. This does not necessarily mean Christians will stop attending church or believing Christian doctrines. Rather, practical atheism undermines Christianity at a more fundamental level by endowing Christians with habits, dispositions, and a vision of reality that is incompatible with embodying the Christian faith. According to John Paul II, "Entire groups of the baptized have lost a living sense of the faith," and "live a life far removed from Christ and his Gospel."[86]

Determining the extent to which modern culture is secular—and whether Christians have unwitting internalized secular dispositions—requires an assessment that goes deeper than survey analysis or genealogies of the secular. What is needed instead is an analysis of the underlying *form* of modern social structure and culture.[87] James K. A. Smith calls Christians to "'read' the practices of the regnant polis, to exegete the liturgies of the earthly city in which we are immersed."[88] To that end, what is the underlying logic of the dominant social practices of the modern age? What kinds of dispositions are fostered by these practices? Do these dispositions effectively turn practicing Christians into practical atheists? The following chapters will explore key social practices related to education, work, consumption, and leisure to assess whether they are rooted in an underlying secular form that shapes people in ways that are incompatible with the Christian life.

---

86. John Paul II, *Redemporis Missio*, sec. 33.

87. John Paul II also calls for an assessment of whether modern social structures foster "participation" or "alienation," saying they "absolutely must be evaluated in light of this basic criterion: do they create [these] conditions—for this is their only real function." Wojtyla, *Person and Community*, 206.

88. Smith, *Awaiting the King*, 195.

―― 2 ――

Education

MANY CHRISTIANS VIEW EDUCATION as an important battleground in their fight against encroaching secularism. Christian parents are wary of public education, suspecting that bad peer influence and teachers who challenge religion will lead their children astray. Underlying these fears is the assumption that exposure to false and misleading ideas could weaken their children's faith.

Exposure to such ideas can certainly be secularizing, but many parents see this as the only way education challenges the faith of their children. This is mistaken for two reasons. First, overt challenges to Christianity could strengthen students' faith by motivating them to better understand and defend what they believe[1]—at least for those with a strong foundation. Exposure to anti-Christian sentiment is not optimal, but it does not necessarily undermine religious faith. Second, social influence occurs primarily through practices that cultivate enduring dispositions—not just ideas delivered from the front of a classroom. After all, being a Christian is more than holding the right beliefs, but involves growing in the necessary virtues of the Christian life. Therefore, parents should not only concern themselves with whether their children are exposed to content that contradicts Christianity, but they must question whether the educational practices of school itself indirectly foster secular dispositions of mind and heart. How do the

---

1. This is consistent with Christian Smith et al.'s findings about the evangelical subculture in *American Evangelicalism* (104–16).

practices of modern education, which permeate both public and Christian schools, govern how students envision reality?

Modern Approaches to Education

Modern approaches to education have become so widely accepted that it may be difficult to appreciate their formative power. Yet many of the hallmarks of modern education are relatively new inventions, including grades, grade point averages, majors, and scholarships. The first universities were founded in Europe around the twelfth century and sought to better understand how the world and human life related to God.[2] Higher education in the United States also began as an overtly religious endeavor. Harvard's original mission was for students to realize that the "main end of [one's] life and studies is to know God and Jesus Christ which is eternal life."[3] Even the first public universities in the United States embraced the influence of religious faith. One study of twenty-four public universities found that twenty-two still offered (and sometimes required) chapel services in 1890, and four even required Sunday church attendance.[4]

Even though religion remained a force in higher education well into the nineteenth century, a new model of education based on the German research university began to gain prominence. This new approach privileged the creation of knowledge through the scientific method (which became the standard of truth) over the time-honored pursuit of immeasurable truth, beauty, and goodness—which became seen as merely subjective, and was no longer prioritized in many curricula. This new model reimagined and reorganized education around practical ends, revolutionizing the organization of the curriculum, course content, and teaching methods. Alasdair MacIntyre notes, "Research universities in the early twenty-first century are wonderfully successful business corporations subsidized by tax exemptions and exhibiting all the acquisitive ambitions of such corporations."[5]

On the surface, prioritizing practical skills and knowledge may seem best. After all, the United States is a pluralistic society, meaning its overt support of any foundational truth would seem to infringe on *some* religious perspective or worldview. Respecting everyone's freedom of belief seems to

2. Glanzer et al., *Restoring the Soul of the University*, 28–31.
3. Harvard GSAS Christian Community, "Shield and Veritas History," para. 2.
4. Marsden, "Soul of the American University."
5. MacIntyre, *God, Philosophy, Universities*, 174.

imply that public education should ignore religious questions. Since people cannot agree on the truth of reality, perhaps education should only address knowledge that prepares students for their future careers, no matter their religious or philosophical commitments. Though this may seem like a commonsense compromise that benefits both Christians and non-Christians, this approach is not neutral since it inevitably privileges and reinforces some vision of the created order, freedom, and the good life. By distancing itself from transcendence, modern education embraces the assumption that only what is measurable counts as true knowledge, which lends itself to teaching methods and topics that have a clear application.

The arts and humanities may still find a place in modern education, but they have been repurposed as tools for developing practical skills such as creativity or reading comprehension. Philosophy courses are no longer treated as the pursuit of wisdom rooted in learning for its own sake, but seen as a means to improve "critical thinking."[6] Even if modern education does not overtly state that reality is defined by what is measurable, it implicitly treats religious and philosophical truth as private matters, while exalting usefulness as the highest end of education. This perpetuates a vision of reality where the created order is merely raw material—inherently meaningless until put to use. Students are free to hold private beliefs about the deeper meaning and purpose of creation, but these are effectively ignored—and even contradicted—by the underlying assumptions and methods of modern education.

Rejecting the inherent meaning of creation enables modern education to envision nature itself as something to be controlled, used, and ultimately overcome. This reflects the false notion that freedom is achieved when humanity imposes its will without limits—"freedom from" restraint—rather than the true freedom of living in accord with the truth of reality.[7] God has given the world for people's use, but exercising dominion in a way that does not devolve into a sinful form of domination requires a deeper understanding of the meaning of the created world and the purpose of life. Tragically, such questions are effectively ignored by modern education, rather than treated as foundational.

This false notion of freedom also perpetuates a misleading vision of human flourishing. On the surface modern education might seem neutral toward human flourishing since it does not specify how students ought

---

6. Adler, *Battle of the Classics*, 23–28.
7. Berlin, "Two Concepts of Liberty."

to live. Yet the system defines success in terms of grades, test scores, and college placement, which are achieved by learning to efficiently acquire practical knowledge. In this way, modern education rewards students who demonstrate the highest potential for economic productivity, which signals that career success—and the lifestyle it enables—are the primary determinants of a good life. Just browse the alumni magazine from any college or university to see these assumptions on full display. Alumni who land prestigious jobs and promotions are worthy of mention, while other stories tout how the institution is preparing the next generation of students for even greater success.[8]

Reducing education to the lowest common denominator of career preparation is not religiously neutral, but fosters a vision of reality that contradicts a Christian vision of creation, the purpose of life, and what it means to live well. Christians may claim to reject these underlying assumptions and strive to supplement practical learning with religious perspectives, but their efforts occur within an educational ecology that marginalizes higher forms of knowledge. The Department of Education, accrediting bodies, and states devise educational policies in light of the needs of the economy, dictating how schools and teachers must operate. What sorts of skills, knowledge, and abilities are needed for today's students to become tomorrow's workforce? This produces an environment where academic success is defined in terms of career preparation. For schools to maintain enrollment in this environment they must meet the expectations of parents, policy makers, and future colleges or employers, which informs their decisions related to hiring, course offerings, methods of instruction, and the use of technology.

The Formative Practices of Modern Education

These underlying assumptions related to creation, freedom, and the good life are not readily apparent in mission statements and school brochures, but instead are manifested and perpetuated through the routines of the typical school day. Prevailing methods of instruction may seem neutral, but they slowly shape how students envision reality. Schools choose from a menu of textbooks that are written with an eye toward basic proficiencies, outcomes, or objectives. Textbook reading is often supplemented by in-class

---

8. This is not to say that colleges and universities are only concerned with career success, but alumni magazines imply that this is most important.

PowerPoint lectures supplied by the textbook's publisher. These methods of information delivery are so widespread that many schools could hardly operate without them. Though they are unlikely to foster a love of learning, these methods remain prevalent because they are a highly efficient means of relaying basic information on any given topic, which reflects the assumption that the purpose of education is to fill students with useful facts.

This model of education enables the creation of grade-specific benchmarks for reading, math, and science, which have become the standard of success for teachers, schools, and even entire states. Teachers are tasked with efficiently transmitting information to students and assessing their retention—often through multiple choice exams—which become interpreted as a measure of intelligence, work ethic, and one's qualification for college admission or employment. This method of education and assessment is reinforced by the importance adults grant to these educational practices. Principals and teachers celebrate when aggregate test scores and levels of proficiency improve their school's overall rating. Parents proudly share when their children are reading or doing math above their grade level. Students learn what is required to succeed within this framework, enabling them to gain admission to college and be awarded scholarships. Employers hire workers who are savvy enough to navigate the bureaucracy of modern education.

For many students, the practices of reading textbooks, listening to lectures, taking multiple choice exams, and receiving letter grades are synonymous with education. Teachers and administrators value these practices because they are efficient and quantifiable. Even though leading students through pre-prepared materials may seem commercialized and impersonal, it appears relatively benign on the surface. After all, learning certainly happens in such an environment. But what kind of learning? Parents, teachers, and administrators may be satisfied with this arrangement, but Christians should question how this approach shapes their children's vision of reality. What dispositions of mind and heart are fostered through educational practices that ignore transcendent truth? Is such an education conducive to fully embodying the gospel within one's future life and career?

Forming a Secular Imagination in the Classroom

The exaltation of efficiency and practicality effectively crowds out knowledge that is not readily measurable or useful, and thereby initiates students into one-dimensional ways of thinking that obscures a more comprehensive

Education

vision of reality. Christians should grant priority to qualitative forms of knowledge, especially since truth, beauty, and goodness cannot be quantified. Leading students to recognize and love what is true, beautiful, and good should be the primary purpose of education, yet modern forms of education hinder this end by relying on educational practices that are unable to convey the richness and depth of reality.

Another effect of exalting efficiency and practicality is that students are implicitly taught to overemphasize educational outcomes—earning grades and a credential—but devalue the process itself. Many students are only concerned with learning enough to earn grades and their degree, rather than seeking transformation. Some may experience personal change through their education, but this is more likely due to experiences outside of the classroom, such as study groups, office hours, or projects. What should be an initiation into a lifelong process of learning—for its own sake—by joining a community of learners, has become an exercise in efficiently checking the boxes needed to gain a credential.

This does not mean students are completely apathetic toward education. Despite their indifference toward learning itself, many students remain hyperfocused on the measurable outcome of their grade, with research suggesting that 50 to 70 percent of college students engage in some form of academic dishonesty (e.g., cheating on a test, plagiarism) during their academic careers.[9] Of course, cheating is frowned upon and severely punished. Nor is it necessary for success. But ironically academic dishonesty is consistent with the way modern education privileges outcomes over process, since students who cheat are committed to achieving the outcome of a grade with little regard for the process of learning. In recent years "study" sites such as Quizlet and Course Hero have grown in popularity, allowing students to post lecture notes, flashcards, and even test questions. Students who rely on these websites may temporarily retain enough information to pass their classes, but it is questionable whether they have truly learned the course content. Should teachers and administrations really be surprised that students have learned to game the system in a way that is consistent with the results-oriented logic that pervades modern education?[10]

9. Hamlin et al., "Comparison of University Efforts," 35.

10. In Weberian language, students have developed a "practical rationality" that is consistent with the "substantive rationality" (i.e., values) of modern education, in a way that may not technically transgress its "formal rationality" (rules, regulations, and laws). For a more detailed discussion of Weber's concepts of rationality see Kalberg, "Max Weber's Types," 1151–59.

Practicing Christians, Practical Atheists

The prevalence of academic dishonesty is consistent with the findings from Christian Smith's study of adolescents and young adults, which found that few students could envision a purpose for education beyond its instrumental use.[11] Even at Christian colleges, many have adopted an instrumental view of courses in history, literature, and philosophy, seeing them as something to "get out of the way" before beginning one's major. This box-checking mentality does not merely describe a handful of bored freshmen, but characterizes how many students, parents, and even advisors perceive courses in the core curriculum. One professor at a Christian liberal arts college asks freshmen from a required core class how many of them would continue to attend college if they could have the job of their choice without finishing their degree. In classes of forty students only a few raise their hands each semester.[12] This anecdote is consistent with the increasing number of students who are entering professional degree programs in healthcare, engineering, or criminal justice, instead of choosing a major in the humanities.[13]

Even many universities treat education instrumentally, reducing their core curriculum and cutting humanities majors and faculty positions to reduce costs. These actions reveal many universities' underlying vision of education: the humanities may be useful for broadening students' perspectives or encouraging critical thinking, but ultimately they are seen as less essential for preparing students for economic productivity. Professional degrees and practical learning are not inherently bad, but they must find their proper place within an approach to education that prioritizes the highest truths.

Modern education does not prohibit students from intending to envision the world through a Christian lens, but its methods and assumptions imply that such beliefs are private and have no real connection to the "real world" of business, politics, and other aspects of public life. Students may be able to incorporate their private beliefs into public settings in small ways: wearing a cross, hosting a lunchtime Bible study, or mentioning God during a class discussion. But these are relatively trivial compared to the force of the dominant social imaginary fostered throughout modern education. Students may intend to "do all to the glory of God" (1 Cor 10:31), aspiring to be servant-leaders in the workplace, while treating their work as a means of supporting their local congregation or world missions. These

---

11. Smith and Snell, *Souls in Transition*, 54.
12. This anecdote is courtesy of an acquaintance of mine.
13. Nietzel, "Whither the Humanities," para. 16.

are certainly good things. Yet even students with these good intentions participate in a system that fosters secularity of mind by inviting them to treat education, work, and the created world as inherently void of meaning and purpose. How does this instrumentalizing mindset relate to Christians' lived faith? Some may concede that the "box-checking" mentality is regrettable, but is it really detrimental to the Christian faith? What becomes of Christian students who intend to devote their careers to God's glory, but attend schools that train them to treat the world instrumentally?

Secularity of Mind

This box-checking mentality reveals that many students envision their education almost exclusively in terms of its *this-worldly* applications and benefits. This prevents students from envisioning truth, beauty, and goodness within the world, thereby hindering their ability to align their lives with *other-worldly* reality. Literature should not only be read by English majors or to improve reading skills, but because it provides a window into the truth of reality. The box-checking mentality that pervades modern education reflects a secular vision of reality, which further habituates students to become overly concerned with *this-worldly* success.

This secularity of mind does not necessarily mean students will stop attending church or believing in God. Yet people's ability to love and worship God depends to some extent on being able to envision the fullness of reality and conform one's life to it. By offering a shallow and incomplete vision of the world, modern education obscures God's presence and goodness. This is consistent with John Paul II's critique of the culture of death, which is characterized by a "loss of contact with God's wise design,"[14] where "nature itself, from being 'mater' (mother), is now reduced to being 'matter,'" and is "subjected to every kind of manipulation."[15]

This reduction of nature (mater) to mere matter is a defining feature of modern education. According to John Paul II, losing sight of God's wise design is a step toward secularization because it leads to an "eclipse of the sense of God."[16] By losing the ability to envision God's presence in the world people begin "living as if God did not exist,"[17] even if they continue to believe

14. John Paul II, *Evangelium Vitae*, sec. 22.
15. John Paul II, *Evangelium Vitae*, sec. 22.
16. John Paul II, *Evangelium Vitae*, sec. 21.
17. John Paul II, *Evangelium Vitae*, sec. 21.

in God. John Paul II states, "It is clear that the loss of contact with God's wise design is the deepest root of modern man's confusion."[18] This is "the deepest [root] of the struggle between the 'culture of life' and the 'culture of death,'" which characterizes "a social and cultural climate dominated by secularism."[19] Even Christian students with lofty aspirations and good intentions may internalize a disenchanted, secular vision of reality. How can they become the kind of people who delight in truth and goodness if they are unable to envision God's presence in the world?

Integrating the Christian Faith into Modern Education

This critique clearly applies to many forms of public education, but what about Christian schools that claim to seek truth and wisdom? Research shows that after accounting for factors such as parents' religiosity, Christian education only results in small increases in the religiosity of students during adolescence and into young adulthood. Catholic students are generally no more religious than students at public schools after accounting for parents' religiosity, while students from Protestant schools were more likely to practice prayer and claim that their faith was important to them and guided their decision-making.[20] Ultimately the effects of Christian education are unclear, since much of the measurable difference between students attending Christian and non-Christian schools can be traced to other factors, such as the presence of religious peer groups and mentors.[21]

Being a Christian means more than attending church or believing in God, however, and studies that rely on superficial measures of religiosity ultimately reveal little about whether Christian education is deeply formative. A more nuanced approach must assess whether students have experienced a transformation of mind or internalized secular dispositions of mind and heart. Do Christian schools truly transform students' minds, or do they unintentionally perpetuate a secular vision of reality?

The answer to this question depends on how Christian educators integrate faith and learning. Many Christian schools regularly pray before class, devote time during the school week to Mass or chapel, and require courses

---

18. John Paul II, *Evangelium Vitae*, sec. 21.

19. John Paul II, *Evangelium Vitae*, sec. 21.

20. Uecker, "Catholic Schooling," 360–64; Uecker, "Alternative Schooling Strategies," 576–79.

21. Uecker, "Alternative Schooling Strategies," 576–79.

in theology. Some teachers share their personal faith, disciple students, or imagine their work as servant-leadership with fellow brothers and sisters in Christ. Courses in history, literature, or science may highlight Christian themes and incorporate Scripture and theology. These are all good things, but these methods of integrating faith could merely be *additions* to a method of education that is otherwise indistinguishable from secular approaches.[22] Does the mere addition of Christian elements enable students to be "transformed by the renewal of [their] mind" (Rom 12:2) if the school otherwise embraces modern curricula, methods, and standards that are rooted in secular assumptions? How can faith be integrated with learning in such a way as to offset the dominant, secularizing tendencies of modern educational practices?

Even graduates of Christians schools who hold orthodox beliefs and are inspired to continue practicing their faith into adulthood may embody dispositions of heart and mind that are thoroughly secular.[23] Cognitive psychology, the sociology of culture, and philosophical models of human action acknowledge that people's stated beliefs work in tandem with habits and dispositions to shape their behavior, but the latter are arguably more influential.[24] Human action is not solely determined by what people think, but is driven by desires, which have been shaped through a lifetime of practices.[25]

---

22. Glanzer and Alleman, *Idea of Christian Teaching*, 62. Glanzer and Alleman highlight the difference between adding faith to learning and allowing faith to transform learning.

23. David Schindler claims that despite that fact that the vast majority of Americans believe in God, many have "a mind that is no longer intrinsically related to God, however much the heart or the will might remain related." He continues, "The divorce of the mind from holiness—which is to say, the separation of the order of intelligence from God and the loss consequently of an intelligent sense of God—lie at the heart of the contemporary cultural crisis which John Paul II has framed in terms of a growing 'culture of death.'" Schindler, "Order of Intelligence," 419.

24. Haidt, *Happiness Hypothesis*, 4–5. Haidt claims the conscious mind is like the rider of an elephant. The rider may attempt to steer the elephant one way or another, but the elephant is more powerful and may ignore the rider, going wherever it pleases. This does not mean the conscious mind, or our stated intentions, are unimportant. But ultimately human behavior is shaped primarily by our underlying dispositions, and not stated intentions. The rider who wants to control the elephant must channel this intentionality toward training and disciplining the elephant, so that the rider's intentions work in tandem with the elephant's dispositions.

25. Smith, *Desiring the Kingdom*, 81–83.

Christian Education: More than a Name on a Building

Cultivating minds and hearts that are authentically Christian requires a deeper sort of formation—one that cannot peacefully coexist with educational approaches that ignore or marginalize transcendent truth, beauty, and goodness. Instead of adding a few religious elements, a truly Christian education must ensure its curriculum, course content, and teaching methods facilitate a deeper experience of reality and foster growth in wisdom and virtue, rather than merely delivering useful information. This does not mean classes such as science and math are unimportant, but if cultivating a Christian vision of reality truly takes precedence over practical application, then these subjects will be approached from a different perspective. In chemistry class, for instance, the facts of the course content may not change much depending on whether one is Presbyterian, Catholic, or atheist. But integrating faith, including the particularities of Reformed or Catholic theology, may transform how facts are envisioned within the whole of reality, which could alter its practical application.

By overemphasizing application, modern education invites students to adopt a one-dimensional vision of reality—one that is incapable of revealing the truth of creation and human life. Christians must therefore ensure that the method of education corresponds to the truth of each topic. What methodological approaches are capable of revealing the truth in a world that is full of God's grace and should ultimately be directed to his glory? Consider how a typical biology class teaches students about cells by focusing on their basic structure and function. Such an approach reveals the truth of cells, but only in one dimension. A more comprehensive approach might begin by exploring the facts of a cell's structure and function, but becomes multidimensional by studying these facts in light of the whole of reality. For example, a single human cell is as complex as New York City.[26] According to one scientist, "The average cell must utilize close to a million unique adaptive structures and processes—more than the number in a jumbo jet . . . packed into a speck of dust invisible to the naked eye. It is hardly conceivable that anything more complex could be compacted into such a small volume. Moreover, it is a speck-sized jumbo jet which can duplicate itself quite effortlessly."[27]

---

26. Denman, "More Complicated Than New York City," para. 5.
27. Denton, *Nature's Destiny*, 212–13.

Education

Beyond its individual complexity, each cell is harmoniously integrated with surrounding cells and the body as a whole. The human brain is comprised of one hundred billion nerve cells, and each one is connected to tens of thousands of other nerve cells. Every second the brain makes one million new connections between its cells.[28] These facts should elicit awe and wonder, which points toward the deeper meaning of creation and invites us to worship. Joseph Ratzinger (who became Pope Benedict XVI) notes, "Creation is designed in such a way that it is oriented to worship. It fulfills its purpose and assumes its significance when it is lived, ever new, with a view to worship. Creation exists for the sake of worship."[29] If a biology class does not lead students to worship, then its approach may be too one-dimensional, falling short of revealing what creation truly *is*.

A truly transformative education must not merely mimic secular approaches with a few Christian elements sprinkled in for good measure, but should adopt new methods of instruction that are more fitting for introducing students to the fullness of reality in a way that fosters mystery, wonder, and gratitude. This does not mean tools such as PowerPoint lectures and multiple-choice exams have no place in education, but Christian educators must recognize that they are generally inadequate containers for truth, beauty, and goodness. Imagine if beginner dance lessons were taught in a lecture hall with a detailed instruction manual, rather than in a studio through practice. Not only would this approach be unenjoyable, but even if students were to study the manual and pass a multiple-choice exam they would still fail to truly understand dance. Dance cannot be learned, practiced, and loved through lectures and exams, and forcing it into the shape of these teaching methods hinders true knowledge. In the same way, biology, literature, and history are multidimensional areas of study, and Christian educators must go beyond surface-level facts and applications to reveal their deepest meaning and purpose.

One-dimensional science classes are not neutral, but are based on the underlying assumption that people can and should study nature without reference to God. This perspective is agnostic, not neutral, and obscures the fullness of reality. Cells are more than the raw material of life, meaning they cannot be fully understood by only studying their structures and processes: "To understand things is to realize the relationship they have

---

28. Philips, "Introduction," para. 2.
29. Ratzinger, *'In the Beginning,'* 27–28.

to Christ."[30] This does not mean questions related to practical application should be ignored. Some students will devote much time to learning about the mechanical dimension of cells to prepare for careers in healthcare, but these practical applications find their fullest meaning within a multidimensional approach. Only those who "seek first God's kingdom and his righteousness" will be able to understand what cells truly are, in every dimension, allowing "all these things [to be theirs] as well" (Matt 6:33). In other words, Christians must take an approach that grants priority to contemplation (receiving what is) over action, even though contemplation necessarily entails some active response.[31] Christian schools must have the courage to seek first the truth of reality, trusting that God's providence will follow. In this way, "Everything learned and worked for, everything true and beautiful—from whatever source gained—is allowed to be its most full, actual, and beautiful self, in the praise and worship of God."[32]

Schools that strive to offer a truly transformative education may struggle to find a critical mass of students, parents, and teachers who are willing to contradict the status quo. The history of Catholic education serves as an instructive example. Toward the end of the twentieth century Catholic schools became increasingly elite, as 46 percent of students in Catholic secondary schools were from families in the top quarter of income, and 21 percent of seniors in Catholic high schools were not Catholic (up from 2 percent in 1972).[33] These changing demographics were accompanied by a shift in how people envisioned the mission of Catholic education. In one study, fewer than half of Catholic principals identified religious development as their primary mission,[34] while another study found that only 48 percent of Catholic high school teachers said it was essential that Catholic teachings be integrated into the curriculum. Only 22 percent of teachers reported that it is essential for a vast majority of teachers to be Catholic.[35]

The National Catholic Educational Association found that 53 percent of Catholic parents[36] agreed with the statement "Catholic schools place too

---

30. Leclercq, *Love of Learning*, 139.
31. Schindler, *Heart of the World*, 234.
32. Coleman, "For the Sake of Knowing and Loving God," para. 5.
33. Riordan, "Trends in student demography," 33–54.
34. Smith and Denton, *Soul Searching*, 213.
35. Convey, "Perceptions of Catholic Identity."
36. Not only those with children attending Catholic schools.

much emphasis on religious teachings and not enough on academics."[37] They concluded that even though parents see some benefit to a faith-based approach, "A focus on religious instruction alone will not persuade parents to consider a Catholic school for their child."[38] The report advised Catholic schools that "too much (or an above average) emphasis on religious information and visuals will likely reinforce existing perceptions that Catholic schools do not offer a high-quality academic curriculum."[39]

Christian education has established norms for integrating faith and learning, and breaching these norms will surely upset many parents. Rather than offer a thoroughly Christ-centered education, it would be much easier to compartmentalize the faith by fitting chapel (or Mass), prayer, service, and theology into an otherwise secular approach to education. Such schools claim to prioritize wisdom and truth, but their approach could serve to initiate students into a false reality that separates students from the fullness of truth by rendering the Christian faith as an appendage to the primary goal of career advancement. Christian schools will fail to transform their students' minds if their teaching methods functionally "reduce nature (mater) to matter," thereby advancing a worldview where "'quality of life' is interpreted primarily or exclusively as economic efficiency."[40]

Offering a truly transformative education is more than a challenge for schools and families—it is a crisis facing the whole church. A school's success is not defined by test scores, college placement, or athletics, but whether its students are enabled to align their lives with the truth of reality. This is more than an academic exercise, but requires *metanoia*—or transformation of mind.[41] Joseph Ratzinger noted, "The saints were all people of imagination, not functionaries of apparatuses."[42] How can education transform students' minds and facilitate their growth in the Christian life?

A liberal arts education can foster this kind of transformation, even though its purpose is to pursue knowledge for its own sake. Knowing *what is* requires more than the acquisition of facts about the material world, but involves seeing the interconnectedness of all knowledge, including

---

37. National Catholic Educational Association, "Catholic School Choice," 29.
38. National Catholic Educational Association, "Catholic School Choice," 38.
39. National Catholic Educational Association, "Catholic School Choice," 38.
40. John Paul II, *Evangelium Vitae*, sec. 23.
41. Schindler, "Order of Intelligence," 407–28.
42. Ratzinger, *Images of Hope*, 67.

theological truth.[43] The liberal arts are not necessarily intended to form saints.[44] Yet by pursuing knowledge for its own sake students gain an awareness of *what is*, thereby growing closer to God. When education pursues *what is*, it leads students to envision and desire what is truly good and beautiful. This enables them to become people who know and love the source of *what is*—God—rather than merely knowing theological facts and believing in God's existence, but internalizing a thoroughly secular mindset. Does the typical Christian school transform students' minds in this way, enabling them to better know and love God?

Schools may face enough of a challenge trying to form students who intend to continue practicing their faith after graduation. Yet lowering the bar by settling for basic forms of religiosity undermines the depth and beauty of Christianity. After all, being a Christian involves more than a weekend commitment. What good is it to convince people to attend church if they embody a secular vision of reality and live as if God does not exist? It would be better for schools to challenge their students to enter through the narrow gate by introducing them to the radical demands of the gospel than to widen their appeal by offering a simplistic vision of the Christian life.

Christian education is more than a lofty mission statement or a name on a building. Schools whose highest priority is to introduce students to the fullness of reality are rightly called Christian because they prepare students for the only outcome that ultimately matters—sanctity—and they prepare students for postgraduate admittance to the only place that ultimately matters—heaven. What good is it to attend a school that calls itself Christian but whose approach separates students from what is real, even if unintentionally? It would be better to educate students in a way that transforms their minds for sanctity, even if the cost is lower test scores or fewer scholarships. What good is it for students to find career success but become blind to the one thing that could ever satisfy their souls?

---

43. Briel, "University and the Church," 26.

44. John Henry Newman famously states that a liberal arts education "makes not the Christian, not the Catholic, but the gentleman." *Idea of a University*, 91. Newman's point is that a liberal education must pursue knowledge for its own sake, and not be directed toward some other end—even if it is the good end of sanctity. Newman does believe that the pursuit of knowledge for its own sake involves the study of theology, and he does not rule out growing in love of God as a byproduct of seeking *what is*.

3

Work

It is common to ask children, "What do you want to *be* when you grow up?," and one of the first questions adults ask each other when they meet is, "What do you *do*?" These two questions reveal the prominent place of work in our lives. Theological assessments of economics often focus on issues such as stewardship, inequality, and the morality of socialism and capitalism. These are certainly important topics, but Christians must also question how everyday practices related to economics and work shape the Christian life. John Paul II notes that work not only changes the world around us—its objective dimension—but people themselves, or its subjective dimension.[1] John Paul II believed that this subjective dimension is ultimately more important, stating, "It is always man who is the purpose of work."[2]

One way to evaluate modern work is to assess whether it fosters "participation"—communion with others and creation—or "alienation."[3] John Paul II asserts that social structures "absolutely must be evaluated in light of this basic criterion: do they create the conditions—for this is their only real function—for the development of participation?"[4] In his view, this question is "the central problem of life for humanity in our times, perhaps in all times."[5] Since many people spend more waking hours working than

1. John Paul II, *Laborem Exercens*, sec. 6.
2. John Paul II, *Laborem Exercens*, sec. 6.
3. Wojtyla, *Person and Community*, 206.
4. Wojtyla, *Person and Community*, 206.
5. Wojtyla, *Person and Community*, 206.

any other activity,[6] we must ask ourselves, do the practices of modern work foster participation or alienation? What sorts of dispositions are cultivated by modern approaches to work? How does work shape people's souls?

The Landscape of Modern Work

How and why people work has radically changed in the modern age. In 1850, 64 percent of Americans were farmers, but today only 2 percent of the population is needed to produce an overabundance of food.[7] Nearly every industry has witnessed such gains in productivity, as everything from food to home construction has become subject to new models of mass production based on the scientific management of employees and work processes.[8] In the early days of mass production people imagined that long work hours would inevitably be replaced with leisure, as new technologies could easily provide for people's basic needs in less time. Instead, increases in productivity allowed the middle class to acquire items that were once considered luxuries, such as refrigerators, automobiles, and even indoor plumbing. Rather than working less, people began to work more as they pursued new consumer goods that became equated with the American dream.[9]

These new approaches to production exalted the principles of efficiency, predictability, calculability, and control.[10] McDonald's applied these principles to food production, which essentially invented the fast food industry and revolutionized American life in the process. Efficiency and control are crucial in today's highly competitive food industry. One study found that reducing the wait time in the drive-thru by just seven seconds would lead to a 1 percent increase in market share.[11] Every step of the growth, delivery, storage, and assembly of food must be subject to scrutiny. Potatoes are custom bred for French fries, and naturally fluctuating levels of sugar (based on when potatoes are harvested) are held constant through

---

6. Bureau of Labor Statistics, "Average hours."

7. Associated Press, "Farm Population Lowest Since 1850's."

8. Miller, *Consuming Religion*, 39–46. Miller provides a helpful description of Fordism and Taylor's approach to scientific management.

9. Schor, *Overworked American*, 78.

10. Ritzer, *McDonaldization of Society*, 16–18.

11. Gwynne, "Customer's Time," para. 1.

seasonal adjustments.[12] This level of control may seem excessive, but even small increases in efficiency help reduce costs and maximize profit.

These principles not only govern factory work and fast food, but nearly all sectors of professional life, even education and ministry, are becoming "McDonaldized" as they seek greater efficiency and control.[13] On the surface, the wide-scale adoption of these principles has led to great success by enabling people to do more with less, as both corporations and nonprofits have become increasingly efficient and intentional as they provide goods and services for customers and stakeholders. This emphasis on efficiency and control triggered economic growth and massive profits, which are a good indicator of whether a business is meeting people's needs.[14] Though John Paul II praises how modern markets "help to utilize resources better . . . [promoting] the exchange of products,"[15] he also emphasizes that work must be organized in ways that are consistent with the fullness of people's humanity.[16] John Paul II calls for a holistic assessment of the economy, claiming that it "must be guided by a comprehensive picture of man which respects all the dimensions of his being and which subordinates his material and instinctive dimensions to his interior and spiritual ones."[17] When the economy is not organized in this way, the result is "often damaging to [people's] physical and spiritual health."[18] There is no question that modern forms of production have raised people's material standard of living, but how does this emphasis on efficiency and profit influence workers and consumers themselves?

Efficiency, Commodification, and True Value

In general, the modern market is agnostic toward higher goods. In some cases, the government may step in to prohibit the sale of goods or services—such

---

12. Schlosser, *Fast Food Nation*, 130.

13. Drane, *McDonaldization of the Church*, 45. Drane describes how the principles of McDonaldization have distorted the church's approach to ministry. This will be discussed at length in chapter 7.

14. John Paul II, *Centesimus Annus*, sec. 35. Even though John Paul II is sometimes critical of capitalism, he acknowledges its benefits as well.

15. John Paul II, *Centesimus Annus*, sec. 40.

16. John Paul II, *Laborem Exercens*, sec. 6.

17. John Paul II, *Centesimus Annus*, sec. 36.

18. John Paul II, *Centesimus Annus*, sec. 36.

as body organs or sex—but generally value is imputed solely on the basis of supply and demand. Of course, Christians are free to refrain from working in industries or engaging in economic transactions that offend their personal morality, but the system itself appears to be neutral. Some Christian apologists of the free market see this as one of the virtues of a free society: everyone has the freedom to buy and sell based on their personal conscience, except in cases of overt immorality that contradict natural law.[19]

Yet this defense does not account for the subjective effects of work: how work itself shapes people themselves. Modern work seeks to maximize efficiency. While efficiency is good in principle, John Paul II claims that the exaltation of efficiency is dehumanizing "when it is organized so as to ensure maximum returns and profits with no concern whether the worker, through his own labor, grows or diminishes as a person . . . in which he is considered only a means and not an end."[20] In other words, efficiency must never be achieved at the expense of the inherent dignity, purpose, and meaning of human life. Does the modern economy foster an environment where individuals and firms can prioritize these higher ends?

Without a clear vision of the deeper meaning and purpose of creation and human life, the exaltation of efficiency inevitably leads to commodification—treating nature and human beings as mere inputs in an economic process. Early observers of American society, including Alexis de Tocqueville and Max Weber, witnessed an American tendency to treat the natural world primarily as a means to make money.[21] De Tocqueville noted, "Americans measure the value of all things solely in terms of the answer to the following question: How much money will it bring in?"[22] Since profit margins can be incredibly narrow, businesses seeking to make a profit are incentivized to treat nature and other human beings—both their workers and customers—as mere commodities, who must first be seen in terms of their role in the process of production and consumption.

Consider how chickens are manufactured through a highly controlled process that treats animals as mere commodities. Meat producers choose from among species of chicken that are bred specifically for consumers' tastes and needs.[23] In the 1960s, it took sixty-five days for chickens to grow

19. Novak, *Spirit of Democratic Capitalism*, 53–54.
20. John Paul II, *Centesimus Annus*, sec. 41.
21. Nolan Jr., *What They Saw*, 211–14.
22. As cited in Nolan Jr., *What They Saw*, 273n50.
23. Purdy, "Designing fatter birds," para. 3.

to 3.5 pounds, but today it only takes forty-seven days for them to reach six pounds.[24] These chickens grow so quickly that they can hardly walk, because their legs cannot accommodate this rapid weight gain.[25] Consumers appreciate lower prices at the grocery store, but they are neatly separated from the ugly side effects of commodification that make low prices possible. This approach may reduce the cost of chicken, but it relies on one of the hallmarks of the culture of death: "nature (mater) being reduced to matter."[26]

The drive to increase profits by maximizing efficiency also incentivizes businesses to envision workers and customers as commodities. Producers increase their chances of being profitable if they can find cheaper labor without sacrificing quality. Some corporations, such as Walmart, have historically preferred to pay a lower wage, while accepting the consequences of higher employee turnover and lower quality work.[27] Customers are also commodified when they are treated merely as consumers. Businesses do not question how much of their product is necessary for a good life—or whether it is necessary at all. Rather, they are motivated to sell as much as they can convince people to buy. John Paul II notes how this mindset is dehumanizing: "When man is seen more as a producer or consumer of goods than as a subject who produces and consumes in order to live, then economic freedom loses its necessary relationship to the human person and ends up alienating and oppressing him."[28] This tendency to treat employees and customers as commodities cannot be attributed solely to the individual greediness of managers and executives, but is consistent with the internal logic of an economic system that obscures the deeper spiritual meaning of creation and human life.

The Hidden Costs of Commodification

Despite this pervasive commodification, some praise the ability of modern economies to keep costs low—making products available to more people. Costs may be kept low—but only in a limited, short-term sense. A full assessment of the modern economy must also account for costs that are not directly incurred by producers or consumers—what economists call

24. Purdy, "Designing fatter birds," para. 6.
25. Keim, "Farmed Chickens Can't Walk," para. 1.
26. John Paul II, *Evangelium Vitae*, sec. 22.
27. Cascio, "High Cost of Low Wages," para. 5.
28. John Paul II, *Centesimus Annus*, sec. 39.

"negative externalities." For example, producers keep the monetary cost of food relatively low by passing on the true cost to consumers in the form of health and food safety issues. The mass production of chicken increases the risk of contamination, as one study found that two out of three chickens purchased in grocery stores were contaminated with salmonella or campylobacter bacteria, which could sicken people if not handled properly.[29] Another study found that air pollution from modern farming techniques could contribute to over seventeen thousand deaths per year in the United States.[30] Lower costs also allow people to consume meat more often—perhaps more than we should. Eating meat in moderation is beneficial, but the average American eats 110 pounds of red meat per year,[31] which is linked to obesity.[32]

The US government also treats food as a mere commodity, which further contributes to unhealthy eating habits by incentivizing farmers to grow as much food as possible, without much regard for whether it is truly needed. As a result, an additional seven hundred calories of food per person is produced every day.[33] To profit from this overabundance of food, corporations seek to artificially increase people's food consumption through marketing and providing food in more stores and public places. These practices nudge people toward overconsumption,[34] which contributes to the fact that nearly three out of four Americans are now obese or overweight.[35] Annual healthcare costs in the United States now approach $12,000 per person[36]—nearly twice that of other Western countries. This warrants a reassessment of the commodification of food: are the benefits of cheap food worth its high cost?

Perhaps the most important "negative externality" of commodification is its spiritual cost. Treating creation—food, soil, and animals—as mere raw material for the modern food system separates people from the inherent goodness of the created world. In other words, commodification perpetuates a culture of death by furthering a "loss of contact with God's wise design,"[37]

---

29. Dorning, "Consumer Reports," para 1.
30. Kaplan, "Air pollution," para 2.
31. National Chicken Council, "Consumption of Poultry and Livestock," see table.
32. Wang and Beydoun, "Meat Consumption."
33. Nestle and Nesheim, *Why Calories Count*, 180.
34. Nestle and Nesheim, *Why Calories Count*, 154.
35. Centers for Disease Control and Prevention, "Obesity and Overweight," para. 1.
36. Wager et al., "Health spending," para 3.
37. John Paul II, *Evangelium Vitae*, sec. 22.

obscuring our "sense of God" and his goodness in the world. The world itself is God's sacrament—offering people a chance to experience creation as a grace-filled gift and respond with gratitude for God's abundant goodness.[38] In the past, people were more inclined to eat with a spirit of festivity and gratitude since they could only afford to eat meat on special occasions or feast days. Today's consumers may be able to purchase boneless chicken breast for two dollars per pound, but they may fail to fully appreciate its goodness since they can consume it at nearly every meal. These hidden costs, whether physical or spiritual, result from what John Paul II criticized as "an 'idolatry' of the market, an idolatry which ignores the existence of goods which by their nature are not and cannot be mere commodities."[39]

Christian Resistance to Commodification

Of course, Christians may object to these forms of commodification. But this does not change the fact that most Western Christians live and work within a culture of death that exalts efficiency and profit, which shapes their vision of reality in ways they fail to realize. How free are Christians to resist the commodifying tendencies of the modern economy? The answer depends in part on the underlying moral order embedded within our economy, and the workplace more specifically. The sociologist Robert Jackall studied the corporate workplace and found a tendency to compartmentalize morality from everyday decision-making. Jackall interviewed one vice president who provided a quote that powerfully summarized his main finding: "What is right in the corporation is not what is right in a man's home or in his church. What is right in the corporation is what the guy above you wants from you. That's what morality is in the corporation."[40] Of course, at the very top of the corporation is the CEO and board of directors, whose primary interest is to maximize profit for shareholders, which requires every input be treated as a commodity for scientific and bureaucratic management.

Jackall also found the key to advancing in the modern corporation is not necessarily knowledge or skill, but adopting the sort of demeanor that is consistent with the ideals and culture of the organization.[41] Well-meaning Christians may be convinced their efforts to bring Christ into the

---

38. Cavanaugh, *Being Consumed*, 53–54.
39. John Paul II, *Centesimus Annus*, sec. 40.
40. Jackall, *Moral Mazes*, 6.
41. Jackall, *Moral Mazes*, 65.

workplace can transform the corporate environment, but their career is dependent on being a "team player" and adopting the ethos of the corporation, which often requires them to privatize their Christian convictions about work, creation, and the human person.

People's struggle to recognize and align their lives with true worth is compounded by the fact that markets tend to flatten all value into monetary terms. The dollar values of income and price are efficient tools that smooth the process of buying and selling labor and goods. But these tools functionally reduce quality to quantity, and have become so dominant that people struggle to imagine true value apart from these artificial indicators.[42] Modern people "know the price of everything, and the value of nothing."[43] John Paul II warned, "If economic life is absolutized, if the production and consumption of goods become the center of social life and society's only value, not subject to any other value, . . . [society] has been weakened."[44] The true value of goods such as nature, silence, prayer, and relationships tend to be underappreciated because their value cannot be captured through a one-dimensional economic lens. Even if Western Christians *believe* money is not true measure of value, they live and work in an economic environment where "'quality of life' is interpreted primarily or exclusively as economic efficiency,"[45] which shapes how they envision reality.

Alienation from Self-Worth

This economic mindset also distorts how people envision their own worth and identity. The United States is a meritocracy, which leads people to imagine their self-worth in terms of success—often defined by one's income and job title.[46] In the past, people's sense of self was tied to their family, church, or community—rather than being a product of their own creation. At the very least identity was rooted in something more enduring, such as one's character. Now 83 percent claim work is an "important source of their basic sense of worth as a person."[47] Modern society may offer a wide variety of avenues for self-expression and self-creation, but productivity has

---

42. Gay, *Cash Values*, 16.
43. Wilde, *Picture of Dorian Gray*, 35.
44. John Paul II, *Centesimus Annus*, sec. 39.
45. John Paul II, *Evangelium Vitae*, sec. 23.
46. Chen, "Extreme Meritocracy," para. 17.
47. Wuthnow, *God and Mammon*, 31.

become a primary determinant of worth and identity.[48] As a result, people are increasingly depressed as they strive to achieve a secure sense of self.[49] "What do you do?" is a question of "who you are," as people face pressure to treat their career as a primary means for achieving a fulfilling life.

This is not to say that work should be completely irrelevant to people's sense of self. On the contrary, work can enhance people's character and contribute to their identity—at least in some limited way. But our modern economic system ascribes value almost entirely in terms of job title and salary. The result is that loyalty to one's community or employer is secondary to career advancement. Employees are expected to climb the corporate ladder or seek opportunities elsewhere, which prevents them from forming deep and enduring (i.e., decades-long) relationships by rooting their life in a workplace, neighborhood, and church. For this reason, people's careers and community are often too ephemeral to be character-forming in any significant way.[50] Work has become performative, rather than formative,[51] as the meaning and identity available through one's career is due to being promoted and increasing one's salary, rather than developing traits such loyalty, honesty, and reliability. Similarly, blue-collar workers continually face the risk of their jobs being outsourced, and increasingly must turn to the "gig economy" to find work.[52] Both white-collar and blue-collar careers have become a parade of serial relationships with no real commitment beyond the short term. People may treat their work as a major source of identity, but it is unlikely to be character-building when it remains so unstable.[53]

This economic mindset inflates the importance of job title and salary, confusing how people approach some of life's most important decisions. Consider how parents decide whether both spouses will work outside of the home, or if one will stay home to raise their young children. This decision is fraught with tension because paid work offers an objective indicator of value in the form of income, while the exact value of stay-at-home parenting is more difficult to recognize. Deciding whether one spouse will stay

---

48. Max Weber also notes how productivity itself became seen as glorifying to God: "Labor in the service of impersonal social usefulness appear[s] to promote the glory of God and hence to be willed by him." Weber, *Protestant Ethic*, 64.
49. Ehrenberg, *Weariness of the Self*, 3–20.
50. Sennett, *Corrosion of Character*, 15–31.
51. Levin, *Time to Build*, 34.
52. Schor, *After the Gig*, 3–5.
53. Sennett, *Corrosion of Character*, 74.

home requires the ability to properly assess the value of each option. John Paul II's theology of work affirms "the original and irreplaceable meaning of work in the home and in rearing children,"[54] and that "the Church can and should . . . [insist] that the work of women in the home be recognized and respected by all in its irreplaceable value."[55] Even if families agree with these principles, their decision may still be fraught with mixed emotions if they have been conditioned to assign value primarily through the lens of price tags and pay stubs. Christian parents may resist this system of endowing value, while still struggling to experience their own worth apart from it.

Stay-at-home parents and children also face pressure to bolster their worth in the eyes of others through productivity. In previous generations, preparing meals and cleaning was full-time work, but modern appliances, prepackaged ingredients, and smart devices have made basic cooking and cleaning less time consuming. Paradoxically, these technologies have not carved out more time and space for rest, prayer, and personal relationships, but instead raised the standard for what constitutes a clean and fashionable home. The condition of the home has become a status symbol, providing stay-at-home parents with a way to produce something of value in others' eyes. Pristine photos of meals and home décor are frequently shared on social media, portraying a false sense of reality—and other people's productivity. The deepest meaning and purpose of homemaking is to be a gift to one's family, not to display one's ability to stage a home that could be featured in a magazine.

Similarly, children become objectified when parents glorify their ability to be successful in terms of grades, athletic success, and popularity. Most parents would never intentionally withhold their love and affection when their children do not achieve worldly success, but many unwittingly introduce their children to a world where worth is ascribed on the basis of productivity. These signals of success are currency on social media and in the annual Christmas letter, meaning even those who prefer not to compete for social approval still face pressure to match up. This arms race for success encourages over-parenting, while constricting creativity, experimentation, and even the ability to experience failure.[56]

This idolatry of success is perhaps most prevalent in the world of youth sports. In the past, youth sports were a seasonal opportunity to gather

---

54. John Paul II, *Familiaris Consortio*, sec. 23.
55. John Paul II, *Familiaris Consortio*, sec. 23.
56. Esolen, *Ten Ways*, 49–54.

with other children for the purpose of having fun, developing friendships, and building character. Now parents shop around for the best coaches, teams, and private trainers, as their children undertake a yearlong or even childhood-long quest for accolades, including travel teams, high school playing time, and college scholarships. Youth sports have become an idol that demands worship on Sunday morning—or even the entire weekend—as families are required to travel long distances and sacrifice nights and weekends to participate. For many, sports programs are a deciding factor in choosing a high school, and even Christian schools face pressure to boost their enrollment by adopting this hyper-competitive approach. When the Archdiocese of Detroit instructed its elementary and high schools to avoid scheduling athletic events on Sunday, a sportswriter from the *Detroit Free Press* described the move as "idiotic" and claimed the archbishop was "out-of-touch."[57] Children may enjoy sports, but many play in a competitive world they did not create. Not only do young athletes face unnecessary pressure to produce, but both parents and children become further conditioned to imagine worth through the lens of success.

Busyness

This exaltation of productivity results from more than the misplaced values of a few individuals. Rather, an entire system props up this false reality where worth is equated with production. This leads people into chronic busyness, because they can never produce enough to secure a sense of their own self-worth. This is consistent with John Paul II's observation that in a culture of death people are "concerned only with 'doing.'" Even though technological advances and increases in efficiency continue to reduce the amount of work needed to provide for basic needs, true leisure remains elusive. Work now spills over into evenings and weekends, as people send emails from their kid's soccer practice, at the traffic light, and even from bed. People may lament their busyness, but our culture portrays it as a badge of importance.[58]

In response, the market is quick to step in with an apparent solution—inviting people to outsource aspects of their life that they are too busy to attend to themselves (e.g., grocery shopping, cooking, childcare).[59] Like Martha in the gospel, people are busy about many things, but are they

57. McCabe, "War on Athletics," para. 4.
58. Bellezza et al., "Impressed by Busyness," para. 5.
59. Hochschild, *Outsourced Self*, 12.

losing the ability to attend to what truly matters? Many books and seminars promise to alleviate this chronic busyness through various techniques and strategies, but they fail to address the root of the problem: people's inability to experience their own self-worth. John Paul II affirms, "We are not the sum of our weakness and failures; we are the sum of the Father's love for us and our real capacity to become the image of his Son."[60] People have every reason to abandon this desperate quest to experience worthiness through productivity, yet many continue because it remains a commonly accepted means of boosting one's status in today's world.

The Soul-Shaping Influence of Modern Work

Commodification, the loss of a sense of self-worth, and busyness are endemic in modern life, are certainly lamentable, but some may question whether the modern economy is truly to blame. Some may argue that personal responsibility is the solution to these ills, since people have the freedom to resist. Just as people living under oppressive regimes can and do resist, Christians today must have the wisdom and courage to withstand the dehumanizing tendencies of modern life. This narrative of personal responsibility rightly acknowledges the role of freedom and human agency, but it fails to account for how individual choice occurs within a social context that we did not choose and often fail to recognize. Personal responsibility is essential, but the solution is both individual and structural, not either/or. This is evident in the witness of Christians who resisted the oppressive communist regimes of the twentieth century. Such resistance not only required incredible self-determination, but also underground institutions and networks to form people who *could* resist.[61] Such resistance is only likely to occur when people are formed by institutions and practices that make such heroic choices possible.

This chapter's critique aims to uncover how the institutions and practices of modern work are not neutral, but subtly shape the souls of Christians in ways they often fail to realize. Work is not a neutral human activity, since it always occurs within some time and place, and is rooted in some vision of the nature of created order, the purpose of life, and what it means to live well. The modern economy and workplace may seem to be neutral since they make no direct claims regarding whether people

---

60. John Paul II, *Homily*, sec. 5.
61. Dreher, *Live Not By Lies*, 169–70.

believe in God and attend church. Yet they are rooted in the assumption that creation is only raw material, where "nature itself, from being 'mater' (mother), is now reduced to being 'matter,' and is subjected to every kind of manipulation."[62] This social context conditions people to imagine the good life as career success and wealth, and envision other people as competitors or consumers.

Of course, individuals may privately dissent from our culture's distorted vision of creation, dignity, and success. But the modern workplace and economy are governed by the assumption that God's existence and presence are largely irrelevant. In other words, they are rooted in a form of agnosticism that requires Christians to compartmentalize their religious views—leaving them at the door when they enter corporate and professional environments. Christians who are employed in sales cannot imagine their work as discerning with potential customers whether they truly need a particular product and still keep their job. These foundational assumptions of the modern economy are agnostic, and not neutral toward a Christian view of creation and the human person. At best it ignores these essential truths while loudly proclaiming its own false theology—a reality where commodification is the sacrament that makes present the god of wealth.

Resisting this vision of reality is difficult because Christians are embedded within institutions (e.g., schools and workplaces) and surrounded by people, including managers, co-workers, family members, and peers, who affirm (or at least do not overtly challenge) the ways value is imputed primarily through an economic lens. It is difficult for Christians simply to choose to avoid commodification and busyness while actively participating in the practices of modern work, which slowly forms them to envision and embody these principles. Such a vision of reality is not merely misguided, but dehumanizing. Christians rightly stand against this dehumanization when it manifests itself in abortion or euthanasia, but are they aware of how the everyday practices of work can distort their souls?

Truly Good Work

For work to be truly good it must be consistent with the inherent meaning, purpose, and dignity of creation and people. It must not merely have some good effect—such as increasing prosperity—while undermining the truth of reality. Efficiency and utility are good insofar as they do not contradict

---

62. John Paul II, *Evangelium Vitae*, sec. 22.

the truth of creation and the dignity of human people. Truth, not utility, must be the guiding principle of the economy, work, and people's very lives. This is consistent with the Gospel's exhortation to "seek first his kingdom and his righteousness, and all these things shall be yours as well" (Matt 6:33). Work ought to provide for people's material needs such as food and shelter, yet prudence and temperance are required to discern when it is mingled with selfish ambitions and ceases to serve the common good.

Even jobs and careers that seem less glamorous can be ennobling when treated properly. In other words, even if work's objective effects seem insignificant, its subjective effects may have eternal significance. Yet those who exalt efficiency and utility over truth—even when the product of their work is good—ultimately perpetuate an approach to work that undermines the inherent goodness of creation, other people, and themselves. Even if such work is economically productive and successful by worldly standards, it may be dehumanizing if it causes people to lose sight of the dignity of other human beings, and even their own inherent self-worth.

Work is one means through which humans can extend God's love and truth into the world, thereby "sanctifying the world itself to God."[63] Yet this sanctification of the world and our own lives (through God's grace) is only possible by properly ordering work's worldly and higher ends. Adam Smith believed work could only be motivated by the self-interested pursuit of profit, but theologian David Schindler offers an insightful rebuttal. Following John Paul II, he acknowledges that while profit has a legitimate role, its importance must not be exaggerated.[64] Profit is one indicator of when work addresses the needs of others, but it must first be seen as a byproduct of good work, not its highest goal. When profit becomes the primary motivator of people's work it easily becomes an idol that leaves them spiritually bankrupt. De-prioritizing profit does not require people to neglect their material needs, but it does challenge them to question whether they have privileged profit-seeking over other higher ends.

Aiming to embody these principles raises many practical questions. Could a generous gift of self really become the basis of our economy and work? Adam Smith famously quipped, "It is not from the benevolence of the butcher, the brewer, or the baker that we expect our dinner, but from their regard to their own self-interest."[65] Self-interest will always be a fac-

---

63. Second Vatican Council, *Lumen Gentium*, sec. 30.
64. Schindler, *Heart of the World*, 122–26.
65. Smith, *Wealth of Nations*, 12.

tor in people's behavior, but what if it were not the primary motivator of one's work? Imagine a baker who is skilled enough to make high quality bread that truly delights their customers.[66] Even if a baker could increase their profits by baking lower quality bread in a higher quantity, their true self-interest may be to delight their customers, rather than maximize profit. By baking excellent bread, the baker uses the gift of their skill to its full potential. Not only will their customers receive the benefit of higher quality bread, but they would also be enabled to appreciate the personal care, effort, and skill required to bake each loaf. They know the face and heart of the person who baked their bread, allowing them to respond with true gratitude for the God-given gift of the baker's skills.

Even if customers are unaware of the quality of the bread and the care and skill it required, the baker may still enjoy a healthy pride in the excellence of their work. Even if they could have earned additional money by adopting a different approach, the baker is truly richer for doing excellent work and being a gift to others. Contrary to Adam Smith's view of self-interest, the sociologist Michele Lamont found that French lawyers were repulsed by the idea that their work could be treated primarily as an economic transaction, and instead preferred to envision their work as an essential role in service to society.[67] The fact that such differences exist across cultures reveals the possibility of approaches to work that do not exalt money to the detriment of other goods.

Of course, such a baker should rightfully be compensated for their efforts, but in this case profit would not be their sole concern. This example describes an exchange that is more than an economic transaction: the baker and their customers are not merely exchanging money for bread, but experiencing the other's skill or gratitude—and their humanity. Their relationship is not merely economic—but fully human—and thereby mutually enriching in a way that surpasses economic factors. Even if the bakery's price and quality are similar to mass-produced bread, the baker and customer are both richer because they are not alienated from the other. This true wealth may continue to benefit the baker over time, because being motivated by serving others will ultimately be more fulfilling than seeking profit. The baker will be less likely to become bored or resentful toward work, while their customers will have found a person they can trust and actually *want* to reward for their good work.

66. This example is adapted from Schindler, *Heart of the World*, 123–24.
67. Lamont, *Money, Morals, and Manners*, 66.

This baker may even receive some glory through their work. This glory is good, however, because it is found in becoming a gift to others, not in comparison to them. In *The Weight of Glory*, C. S. Lewis argues that our desire for glory is good, because one day we will be glorified in heaven.[68] Our mistake is seeking glory by comparing ourselves to others. When the disciples were arguing over who was the greatest Jesus replied that the greatest should become as the least (Luke 22:26). True greatness is only found in Christ's path to glory: becoming a gift of self to the point of taking up the cross. His path to glory confounded the apostles, but it is the only path to a good life.

We are made in God's image, endowed with inherent worth, and called to this same greatness and glory. But like the apostles, our true worth often eludes us in a world governed by productivity and comparison. Others' success truly poses no threat to us, but this truth is difficult to experience because we have been conditioned to imagine our worth in comparison to others. Many try to achieve self-worth through productivity but end up feeling lowly and inadequate. True glory doesn't require world-class skills or busying ourselves, but the humility of becoming a gift to others. Embracing this vision of a good life is no easy task for people whose hearts and minds are discipled within institutions and practices that dispose them to envision creation, other people, and even their own lives in terms of productivity.

---

68. Lewis, *Weight of Glory*, 39.

4

Consumption

PATTERNS OF CONSUMPTION DISTINGUISH the modern era from every other historical age. For much of human existence the risk was that people would be unable to acquire adequate food, shelter, and other necessary goods, but in today's world modern, industrial nations must question whether their patterns of consumption are sustainable and align with true human flourishing. There is no shortage of critiques of modern greed, affluence, and inequality—from both Christian and secular sources. These are all-important issues that deserve serious consideration. Yet a more important question is how consumerism transforms people's hearts and minds. Consumerism is more than a tendency toward overconsumption, but is embedded within a set of practices that govern how modern people experience the world—forming them into desirers and choosers whose very identity is forged through consumption.

Becoming Desirers, Choosers, Consumers

Our need for food, shelter, and relationships is good and natural. Yet the modern economy is not organized to merely provide for people's basic human needs and offer a few luxuries. Rather, businesses increase their profit and the economy grows when people consume as much as possible. Modern economies must ensure people's desires for consumer goods remain strong—and even increase. John Kenneth Galbraith's theory of consumer demand recognizes that consumption does not cause desire to subside,[1] but rather people's desires are amplified whenever their available choices increase, which occurs when new products are introduced to the market. The more choices people have, the more likely they are to root their identity in what they own—perpetuating an endless cycle of production, desire, and consumption.

Becoming a Desirer

Marketing is the primary means through which businesses stoke people's desires. Advertising invades people's consciousness at every turn, as the average American is exposed to 362 ads per day.[2] Advertising is more than an informative public announcement about a product's features and possible uses. Most advertising is based on the simple narrative that people's lives are incomplete without the product being offered. General Motor's research department conceived of its work as "the organized creation of dissatisfaction."[3] Advertising's purpose is "to increase people's dissatisfaction with any current state of affairs, to create wants, and to exploit the dissatisfactions of the present. [It] must use dissatisfaction to achieve its purpose."[4] Doing so allows businesses to present themselves as the solution to people's problems. One advertisement for Lays potato chips informs people, "It takes 12 muscles to smile, or three simple ingredients: just potatoes, all-natural oil, and a dash of salt." At the bottom of this ad are the words "happiness is simple." Advertising also creates demand by inciting people's greatest insecurities. One marketing firm found that women felt least attractive on Mondays, so they recommended advertising beauty products to women on that day in order to "concentrate media during prime vulnerability moments."[5] Fostering a sense of discontentment allows marketers to offer their product as the solution to people's problems.

The prevalence of advertising leads people to become increasingly skeptical of its claims. The fact that people can no longer be simply persuaded to buy products has caused marketers to adopt a new strategy: instead of inundating people with information about products themselves—followed by a clear sales pitch—advertising fuels people's desires by peddling the lure

1. Galbraith, *Affluent Society*, 144.
2. Johnson, "Daily Ad Exposures," para. 5.
3. Larson, *Naked Consumer*, 20.
4. Lane, *Loss of Happiness*, 179.
5. Rosen, "Grossest Advertising Strategy," para. 3.

of transcendent meaning, purpose, and identity. One marketing consultant suggested corporations should exploit people's hunger for significance and belonging, saying:

> Our enormously productive economy demands that we make consumption our way of life, that we convert the buying and use of goods into rituals, that we seek our spiritual satisfactions, our ego satisfactions, in consumption. The measure of social status, of social acceptance, of prestige, is now to be found in our consumptive patterns. The very meaning and significance of our lives today expressed in consumptive terms. The greater the pressures upon the individual to conform to safe and accepted social standards, the more does he tend to express his aspirations and his individuality in terms of what he wears, drives, eats, his home, his car, his pattern of food serving, his hobbies.[6]

The average American is now exposed to over five thousand brands each day,[7] which leads them to associate brands with a certain ethos, while equipping existing customers to envision their ongoing consumption as an essential component of their style or persona.[8] Advertising offers modern consumers the means to discover and enact their authentic self. The result is that consumption has become a primary source of identity, superceding more traditional sources of meaning, such as one's family, neighborhood, or ethnicity.[9] Even if individual advertisements do not directly increase sales, they offer businesses the opportunity gain long-term customers.[10] Roughly 285 billion dollars are spent each year on advertising in the United States,[11] while all American religious congregations (not only Christian) collect an estimated 84 billion dollars in annual revenue.[12] This means nearly three times as much money is spent spreading the "good news" that consumption can heal our insecurities and make us whole than is devoted to Christian formation in church congregations. No wonder more than 97 percent of Americans can recognize the logos of top corporations—such as Apple,

---

6. Lebow, "Price Competition in 1955," 2.

7. Johnson, "Daily Ad Exposures," para. 4.

8. Campbell, *Romantic Ethic*, 205–6. Campbell's work connects modern consumerism to a romantic ethic of self-creation.

9. Cross, *An All-Consuming Century*, 24.

10. Hollis, "Why Good Advertising Works," para. 5.

11. Guttmann, "U.S. Advertising Industry," para. 1.

12. Grim and Grim, "Socio-Economic Contribution of Religion," 14.

BMW, and Sony[13]—while only 45 percent of Americans could name the four Gospels and 55 percent know the Golden Rule is not one of the Ten Commandments.[14] Corporations view their advertising budget as an essential component of their business model, since it can transform people into lifelong customers by helping them to link their personal identity to various brands.

Such constant exposure to advertising disorders people's desires, which causes them to lose awareness of the need to reorder their desires toward God. This results from everyday practices that characterize modern life, especially engagement with entertainment media, social media, and advertising. Even though people generally try to avoid advertising, their everyday lives are saturated by its images and messaging, which aims to tether human longing to consumer products. Merely reading a magazine, watching television, or using a smart phone (the average American spends more than six hours per day on these latter two activities[15]) provides plenty of exposure to advertising's false promises. Even those who are not a likely customer, or reject the brand's ethos, cannot easily avoid exposure to this messaging that promises to grant fulfillment and a sense of self-worth. These messages become normalized because of their sheer pervasiveness, as well as the fact that other people treat consumer items as granting fulfillment and endowing worth.

Becoming a Chooser

Desire is also inextricably tied to the availability and prevalence of choice. In pre-modern times, people had relatively few choices of how to satisfy their need for food, clothing, and shelter. Today the ways seem innumerable, as the average grocery store carries close to fifty thousand items.[16] Offering choices to satisfy every desire—those we currently have and others we might have in the future—provides businesses more opportunities to increase revenue, leading to economic growth.

This proliferation of choice seems to be the pinnacle of freedom to people living in consumer society. Of course, having choice is good, but only when our capacity to choose exists within a larger moral framework.

13. GraphicSprings, "Most Powerful Logo Survey," see table.
14. Pew Research Center, "U.S. Religious Knowledge Survey," see table.
15. Nielsen, "Time Flies," see table.
16. Malito, "Grocery Stores," para. 6.

Consumption

When and where does choice begin to detract from a life of true flourishing? The answer to this question depends on the nature of freedom. Is true freedom defined by a lack of restraint (negative freedom) or the freedom to attain some good end or purpose (positive freedom)?[17] Freedom from restraint is still necessary and good for achieving some higher end, but this freedom is only rightly understood in light of the purpose and telos of human life and creation itself. John Paul II states, "The manner in which new needs arise and are defined is always marked by a more or less appropriate concept of man and of his true good. A given culture reveals its overall understanding of life through the choices it makes in production and consumption."[18]

Modern consumer society is agnostic toward whether people's choices are truly good, portraying choice itself—without limits—as the highest form of good. When people have more choices, they have more freedom. People do not merely desire items, but choice itself, as they relish the ability to choose between various options, coming to imagine that their final decision will result in lasting satisfaction. Paradoxically, this myriad of choice undermines its apparent benefits. Psychologist Barry Swartz suggests that having more choices is often correlated with lower satisfaction, because our final decision will always be compared with what we could have chosen.[19] The proliferation of choice raises our expectations, which further traps people in a cycle of desire and consumption.

Modern consumer society trains people to imagine that lasting satisfaction can be found within life's many choices. From this perspective, satisfaction and contentment are not primarily a state of being, or the result of living well, regardless of one's circumstances, but can only be found within various options presented by the market. This false vision is perpetuated by modern approaches to shopping. Shopping is alluring not because people enjoy acquiring the items they need (few enjoy grocery shopping), but because there is a certain thrill in choosing something new. This does not mean shopping is bad or that it is wrong to have choices. The problem is that consumer society—including advertising and the shopping experience itself—present choice as an essential component of satisfaction and identity.

The thrill of choosing is so powerful that shopping can be addicting. This is no mere metaphor, but a disorder that is widely recognized in the

---

17. Berlin, "Two Concepts of Liberty."
18. John Paul II, *Centesimus Annus*, sec. 36.
19. Schwartz, *Paradox of Choice*, 99–116.

psychological research on addiction.[20] Shopping has become more than the mere acquisition of life's necessities, but is a social practice with its own self-contained end: the thrill of hunting and choosing items that promise satisfaction. In the past, people's shopping was limited by time and place, since people needed to travel to a physical location where they could only choose from among the available items. But shopping is no longer limited to specific times—or the items in stock in one location—since people can use their phones to order items online from nearly any warehouse across the United States. This approach to shopping is not conducive to a spirit of contentedness—seeking only to obtain what is truly needed from what is readily available. Rather, the practice of shopping itself works to transform people into choosers who are motivated to shop so they can experience the thrill of choosing something new.

As people made in the image of God, our lives are defined by a hunger that can only be satisfied through communion with God. Choice itself does not prevent communion with God, so long as we do not weigh down our choices with the burden of attaining deeper spiritual satisfaction. John Paul II warns how in consumer society, "People are ensnared in a web of false and superficial gratifications rather than being helped to experience their personhood in an authentic and concrete way."[21] Consumer society conditions people to imagine that transcendence, fulfillment, and worth can be found within of the plethora of available choices and lifestyles. No matter what they choose, people are prone to idolatry by placing the weight of deepest longings onto their choices.

Becoming a Consumer

Modern consumer economy not only trains people to become desirers and choosers, but encourages them to construct their personal identity through consumption. But this presents a problem: it would be self-defeating for corporations to offer resources in support of a stable identity, since this would reduce people's need for ongoing consumption. To ensure people's perpetual consumption, products are designed with "planned obsolescence."[22] Many consumer items, especially electronics and vehicles, are intentionally *not* built to last. In a similar way, items such as clothing

---

20. Andreassen et al., "Shopping Addiction," para 2.
21. John Paul II, *Centesimus Annus*, sec. 41.
22. Aladeojebi, "Planned Obsolescence," 1504.

and home décor are subject to the whims of fashion, meaning consumers must regularly discard what is outdated and shop for the latest trends. This encourages people to embrace the role of consumer: always seeking new opportunities and means to affirm their sense of identity.

The perpetual cycle of shopping and discarding consumer items leads people to envision purchases as temporary. Pope Francis critiques this mindset as contributing to a "throwaway culture," which is marked by a mentality of impermanence.[23] Not only is this wasteful and bad for the environment, but it trains people to view the created world as mere commodities that can be employed to satisfy our fleeting desires. A lifetime of participating in this endless process turns people into commodifiers who are unable to experience the truth, depth, and meaning of the created world.

People may object to overconsumption, advertising methods, and the ever-changing norms of fashion, yet these features of consumer society cannot be easily rejected on the basis of one's religious or moral convictions. The reason is that people are initiated into the dispositions of consumerism through the practices of everyday life. In this way, consumer society secularizes people by initiating them into enduring dispositions of heart and mind that are thoroughly worldly. Many have become choosers, with little motivation to reform their desires (and every opportunity to try to fulfill them), who easily lose sight of the true value and purpose of the created world and human life.

Anti-Eucharistic Consumer Society

Even Christians who are critical of greed and consumerism live within a social and cultural context governed by distorted approaches to consumption, which shapes their ability to embody the necessary dispositions and virtues of the Christian life. Of course, many Christians recognize the importance of properly stewarding their money, yet their idea of stewardship does not necessarily prevent them from embodying consumer dispositions, as many compartmentalize their faith from their finances.[24] Money and spending are taboo topics for most Americans,[25] and pastors may be hesitant to challenge this dominant consumer ethos for fear of alienating the people in the pews who otherwise live decent moral lives by today's standards. The

23. Poust, "Throwaway culture," para. 2.
24. Wuthnow, *Poor Richard's Principle*, 299.
25. Wuthnow, *Poor Richard's Principle*, 141–44.

norms of contemporary American Christianity provide a faint boundary to limit consumption, but churches generally fail to offer clear teachings related to money and spending.[26] As a result consumer society is still able to form Christians to become desirers and choosers, whose identity is rooted in their consumption.

The ethos of consumerism stands in stark contrast to the Christian faith, which warns of the dangers of the love of money (1 Tim 6:10). The life of Paul, who discovered the key to true freedom and enjoyment by "learn[ing], in whatever state I am, to be content" (Phil 4:11), stands as a rebuke to this consumer ethos. To grow in freedom and holiness like Paul, Christians must not only struggle against their own tendency toward sin, but they must do so in a culture saturated with false images of fulfillment. The disorder of modern consumerism is clearly contrasted to the kind of consumption Christians practice in the Eucharist. The word *Eucharist* means "thanksgiving," which is fitting since receiving the Eucharist fosters gratitude for the gift of our most essential need: salvation. The Eucharist is also our thanksgiving to God, which further cultivates gratitude as we receive the benefits of its grace in our lives. Modern consumer society reveals itself to be deeply anti-eucharistic, however, since it cultivates dispositions that are deeply antithetical to the grace-filled effects of the Eucharist.

Ingratitude and Impatience

Consumerism forms people to approach the world as consumers driven by manufactured dissatisfaction. This discontentment leaves people less capable of adopting a spirit of gratitude in everyday life, since life's simple pleasures seem to pale in comparison to glitzy consumer goods. Consumerism also promises instant gratification, but the satisfaction it provides is fleeting—leading to a never-ending loop of desire, gratification, and frustration. Consumerism thrives when people restlessly desire and consume with the hope of finding fulfillment. This ingratitude and impatience are more than an unfortunate byproduct of consumerism, but are essential features of most modern economies. By contrast, the celebration of the Eucharist encourages us to long for the coming kingdom.

---

26. Wuthnow, *Poor Richard's Principle*, 326–27; Wuthnow, *God and Mammon*, 121–29.

Consumption

Scarcity, Rather than Abundance

Another effect of consumer society is that people begin to imagine the world as a place of scarcity, rather than abundance.[27] Truly, the world is brimming with goodness and has been given by God to satisfy our needs. Yet the practices of consumer society train people to imagine that this goodness can only be obtained through consumer goods, which are conveniently on sale, but only for a limited time (buy now while supplies last!). The Eucharist is not subject to this scarcity mentality, since it encourages us to receive the never-ending goodness and grace of God that has already been made present. Rather than trying to buy our way to fulfillment, Scripture reminds us of the overflowing abundance of God: "Every one who thirsts, come to the waters; and he who has no money, come, buy and eat! Come, buy wine and milk without money and without price. Why do you spend your money for that which is not bread, and your labor for that which does not satisfy?" (Isa 55:1–2).

Alienation from the Meaning of Creation

The practices of consumer society also hinder people from experiencing the depth and purpose of the created world. The Eucharist is true food: it reveals how the created world is full of meaning, purpose, and goodness, and can be a means of worshiping God and experiencing his grace. But consumer society packages the created world as a mere commodity for satisfying people's desires. Modern production processes obscure their true origin, purpose, and depth of the created world, which fosters a spirit of commodification. This is seen clearly in the example of food. Whole foods such as fruits and vegetables are difficult to brand and advertise, but engineered food products—what journalist Michael Pollan calls "food-like substances"—can be manufactured to meet consumers' demands for foods that are "gluten free," "reduced fat," or "fortified." Every year seventeen thousand new food products hit the shelves,[28] as producers plaster food packaging with claims related to its engineered nutrients. Producing and marketing food on the basis of seemingly fungible nutrients is called "nutritionism." But when nutrients are stripped from whole foods and combined to create highly processed foods they often fail to provide

27. Cavanaugh, *Being Consumed*, 89–94.
28. Pollan, "Unhappy Meals," 65.

the same benefits. One study found that beta carotene in carrots provided excellent health benefits, but when the same beta carotene was used as an additive it had no health benefits, and was even associated with increased risk of cancer.[29] Manufacturers must make a host of adjustments related to sugar, preservatives, and additives to make these manufactured "food-like substances" more palatable. The practices of buying and eating processed food trains people to envision food merely as a manufactured product that acts as a vehicle for delivering various nutrients to their bodies. About 70 percent of the American diet is composed of processed foods,[30] meaning many have grown accustomed to understanding food primarily in terms of ingredients, nutrients, and the claims of advertisers. The result is that many are alienated from food as God's creation.

Membership

This sense of scarcity also describes how we envision our own identity and sense of worth. True identity and worth comes from realizing that we are children of God (1 John 3:2), which is not something that can be bought, earned, or achieved. Yet the modern world offers a false vision of worth and hierarchy. Those who want to be esteemed as worthy must learn to employ commodified consumer goods in a way that expresses a socially desirable persona. The consumer economy ensures this image of worthiness is constantly shifting, meaning only a privileged few can continually attain it—though many try. This pursuit of social acceptance encourages large numbers of people to continually spend themselves—and their money—as they strive to achieve and maintain the latest standards of worthiness.

On the contrary, the Eucharist offers us membership in Christ's body, which ought to be Christians' primary source of identity and community.[31] This membership is no mere voluntary association, but relativizes private ownership in light of the needs of the larger body. Rather than treating consumption as a means of crafting an individual identity, Christians must first understand their right to private property within the context of the needs of the body of Christ, the church.[32] Instead, consumerism encourages

29. Pollan, "Unhappy Meals," 44.
30. Ryssdal, "Processed foods," para. 2.
31. Wirzba, *Food and Faith*, 151–54.
32. Catholic social teaching states, "The *right to private property*, acquired or received in a just way, does not do away with the original gift of the earth to the whole of mankind.

people to envision consumption as a primary means of building identity and fitting in with a certain social class, obscuring the higher purposes and uses of God's gift of creation.

Undermines Communion

Modern consumerism is also anti-eucharistic because it exalts individual desires, while ignoring how these desires create ripple effects that damage our communion with other people and the rest of creation. Modern habits of consumption are made possible by a global system that neatly averts people's attention from dehumanizing working conditions, child labor, the domination and destruction of creation (rather than proper dominion), and the abusive treatment of animals. Rather than fostering communion with all of creation, consumerism separates people from each other, creation, and even their own sense of worth. The world is meant to be a sign of God's grace, but consumerism dis-integrates people from creation and its creator.

Table 1: The Eucharist vs. Anti-Eucharistic Consumer Culture

The Eucharist	Anti-Eucharistic Consumer Culture
Consuming to be consumed by something larger than the self[33]	Consuming for its own sake
Identity through membership in Christ's body	Identity through membership in consumer styles/demographics.
Patiently waiting for the coming kingdom	Seeks instant gratification
Abundance	Scarcity
Act of thanksgiving	Fosters ingratitude

The universal destination of goods remains primordial, even if the promotion of the common good requires respect for the right to private property and its exercise." *Catechism of the Catholic Church*, para. 2403.

33. Cavanaugh, *Being Consumed*, 84.

Table 1: The Eucharist vs. Anti-Eucharistic Consumer Culture

The Eucharist	Anti-Eucharistic Consumer Culture
Communion with others and God	Alienates people from others and the goodness of creation
Grace/freedom to love God	Endless loop of desire and consumption enslaves people to their desires
Relativizes "mine" in light of membership in a body	Emphasizes what is "mine"

In sum, consumerism is anti-eucharistic because it hinders gratitude, abundance, and communion with God and others while fostering ingratitude, scarcity, and alienation. To what extent does this consumer mentality erode our ability to be transformed by the grace of the Eucharist?[34] Receiving the Eucharist is more than an isolated Sunday event—it requires cultivating practices and dispositions where grace can be received into every area of life. Even if someone believes in the transformative power of the Eucharist, its grace may fail to bear fruit if they have been baptized by immersion into the anti-eucharistic mindset of consumerism.

True Religious Freedom

Living in gratitude for God's abundant grace and finding identity and communion in Christ characterizes true freedom. Consumerism masquerades as the pinnacle of freedom, but undermines people's ability to be grateful by rendering them incapable of enjoying the world as they ought. Pursuing freedom from all restriction or limitation—without regard for the purpose and end of human life (positive freedom)—enslaves people to their desires rather than granting them freedom.

Modern society is profoundly anti-eucharistic, yet promises people what seems like freedom: the ability to choose from a myriad of consumer goods that will fulfill their desires and endow them with a secure sense of self. Despite promising individuality and freedom, modern consumerism

---

34. Even if Christians participate in the ceremony of the Eucharist, to some extent their ability to receive its graces is dependent on being properly disposed. See *Catechism of the Catholic Church*, para. 1128.

Consumption

relies on conformity and manipulation. Vendors collect personal information and record people's online habits through websites, loyalty cards, and user profiles, and then sell this data to networks of websites and marketers. Internet marketing draws on a trove of personal data to tailor ads to the preferences of individual users. There are over four thousand data brokering companies worldwide, and the largest one has an average of three thousand data points on over 500 million people.[35] Nearly everything people do online is tracked. One privacy advocate "tracked the trackers" and found that after browsing four mainstream websites over twenty-five different websites were receiving data on his internet usage.[36]

Advertising is the reason Google and Facebook provide entertaining and useful platforms while remaining free of charge. The average Facebook profile is worth an estimated 200 dollars because profile data is regularly bought, sold, and shared for the purpose of tracking and advertising to individual users as they move across the internet.[37] In 2011 more than 300 billion dollars were spent advertising online, which is approximately 1,200 dollars per internet user.[38] Many internet users are unaware of how their data is being used and would likely find these practices to be a disturbing violation of their privacy. Yet websites such as Google, Facebook, and Amazon offer access to information, entertainment, and forms of communication that were never possible in previous times. Even though the internet seems to offer unprecedented freedom, it subjects people to the most unified and pervasive manipulation scheme of all time.

The fact that consumer society masks its manipulation tactics while pretending to offer ultimate freedom reflects what philosopher Michael Hanby describes as a perfect form of totalitarianism.[39] People living under totalitarian regimes (e.g., the Soviet Union) were subject to oppression and control, but at the very least they knew the state was trying to manipulate them—meaning they had the necessary awareness to resist. These governments could only enforce social control through the threat of violence. Modern consumer culture surpasses these totalitarian regimes because it offers people the illusion of ultimate freedom while manipulating their desires. Advertising redirects people's deepest longings and desires for meaning,

---

35. WebFX, "What Are Data Brokers," para. 6.
36. Kovacs, "Tracking Our Online Trackers."
37. Harnett, "Worth to Facebook," para. 12.
38. Madrigal, "Data Worth," para. 4.
39. Hanby, "A More Perfect Absolutism," 26.

purpose, and identity to consumer items. So long as people are fixated on the availability of choice—Coke or Pepsi, iPhone or Android—they fail to realize how they are less free to choose anything but a life of consumption.

This deeper understanding of freedom offers a new perspective on the meaning of religious freedom in society. Even if the law does not prohibit religious belief and practice, Christians' religious freedom is threatened by living in a culture that effectively disables them from embracing the fullness of the gospel within daily life. Of course, society is not directly responsible for forming us to love God and neighbor—and societal religious freedom certainly includes freedom from coercion—but it also relates to whether the conditions of modern society are conducive for living the Christian life. This is consistent with John Paul II's concern that modern society undermines ways of thinking and acting that are essential for living the fullness of the faith. Christianity is more than group membership or a weekend commitment, but a radical call to perfect love (through grace) of God and neighbor (Matt 5:48; Matt 22:37–40). Consumerism restricts people's freedom to embody *this* kind of religion, not through legal means, but by offering membership in a way of life that depicts Christianity as outdated or irrelevant.

Modern consumer society offers the allure of an easy and glamorous path to the good life. Christians may know consumer goods can never satisfy their spiritual hunger, but prolonged exposure to these false images could blur their vision and confuse their hearts, tempting them to look for fulfillment among things of the world. True sight is essential for the Christian life. Jesus said, "The eye is the lamp of the body. So, if your eye is healthy, your whole body will be full of light; but if your eye is not sound, your whole body will be full of darkness. If then the light in you is darkness, how great is the darkness!" (Matt 6:22–23). John Paul II warns, "A civilization that gives such priority, a civilization that is somehow completely focused only on consumption, is a civilization of the 'death of humanity.'"[40] Even if today's Christians maintain belief in God and Sunday church attendance, the practices of modern consumerism work to distort their hearts and blur their vision of reality.

Resisting this dominant consumer ethos and building a eucharistic society requires privileging the *freedom to* do what is truly good (positive freedom) over *freedom from* limitations (negative freedom). This does not mean that negative freedom is unimportant, but that it must be understood

---

40. Wojtyla, *Person and Community*, 272. John Paul II wrote this before he became pope.

within the larger context of positive freedom. To some it may seem that privileging higher goods over individual desires will reduce people's enjoyment and satisfaction of life. On the contrary, learning to be content in all circumstances is what truly empowers people to take pleasure in the goodness of creation. Those who have learned to be content in all circumstances are able to receive the limited enjoyment of earthly things, without turning them into idols. John Paul II once said, "The problem with pornography is not that it shows too much of the person, but that it shows far too little."[41] The same principle applies to modern forms of consumerism: the problem is not that it results in too much pleasure, but too little; the problem is not that it offers too much freedom, but too little. God has given us the world for our benefit, but only those who are free from selfish desires are able to properly enjoy its fruits.

Christians cannot resist consumerism merely through moralizing or philosophical critique, since it disorders their desires and distorts their vision through tangible practices, images, and messages embedded within everyday life. Christians who seek true freedom and happiness must adopt new practices within their families and communities that treat the created world in a way that is consistent with its underlying purpose and meaning as God's creation. John Paul II exhorts, "It is therefore necessary to create life-styles in which the quest for truth, beauty, goodness and communion with others for the sake of common growth are the factors which determine consumer choices, savings and investments."[42] Redeeming choice and consumption requires both avoiding overconsumption and learning to acquire a taste for what is good. Learning to properly enjoy the world, without idolizing its goodness is essential to the Christian life. Yet this path is difficult to find in a consumer society governed by distorted notions of freedom, enjoyment, and the good life.

---

41. As quoted in MacMillan, "Pornography's Technological Handmaiden," 28.
42. John Paul II, *Centesimus Annus*, sec. 36.

5

Leisure and Rest

AS HUMANS OUR LIVES fall into cycles of work and rest. Work is essential to live, but leisure and rest are essential for a life well-lived. To some it might seem that the topic of rest is undeserving of deeper reflection. After all, how people spend their free time seems to be a private matter so long as they avoid overtly immoral activity, since "the Sabbath was made for man" (Mark 2:27). But true leisure relates to more than people's use of their spare time; it becomes a time and place where they pivot from a life of striving, activity, and necessary practical concerns to resting in God's goodness. As the commandment to "keep holy the Sabbath" indicates, Sabbath and leisure are not optional practices, but essential components of the Christian life. Is modern life conducive for leisure and true rest, or does it redirect our souls toward seeking rest in other things?

Sabbath, Leisure, and Learning to Delight

Understanding whether modern social structure and culture foster rest or restlessness requires recovering a deeper understanding of Sabbath and the meaning of leisure. It is widely known that God created the world in six days and rested on the seventh, which might make it seem like the purpose of Sabbath is merely to take a well-deserved break after a long week. Yet God does not need to rest. So why did he? One Jewish commentator suggests creation itself would not be complete without *menuha*, the "rest, tranquility, serenity, and peace of God . . . [which] suggests the sort of happiness and harmony that come from things being as they ought to be."[1] This interpretation demonstrates how Sabbath is far more than taking a well-deserved break, but involves delighting in the goodness of creation.[2] The commandment to "keep holy the Sabbath" is more than practicing self-care in the midst of busyness, but a call to follow God's example of ceasing from work in order to delight in the goodness of creation that already surrounds us.

Practicing Sabbath connects people to one of the foundational truths of the Christian faith: that the created world is a gift from God, given out of love, and brimming with his abundance and goodness. Since God is love and created everything out of love, the reality of the world and our lives can only be truly understood when seen as a gift.[3] A truly Sabbath lifestyle extends beyond Sunday, fulfilling the spirit—and not just the letter—of the command to rest. Sabbath enables people to better enjoy and delight in God's world, yet its practice must be commanded because of the human tendency to forget that life is more than food and drink (Matt 6:25).

This understanding of Sabbath is closely connected to a classical understanding of leisure. Leisure is not just another word for free time. Nor is it mere inactivity. Josef Pieper's foundational book *Leisure: The Basis of Culture* describes how leisure involves ceasing from instrumental activity to receive the goodness of the world.[4] The importance of true leisure can hardly be understated: without leisure, we risk losing the ability to offer worship to God in and through our daily lives, which will otherwise become governed by a mentality of total work. True leisure fosters worship by allowing us to glorify God—returning the goodness of the world to him through its proper use, enjoyment, and thanksgiving.[5]

Practicing Sabbath and prioritizing leisure enables people to recognize that God has provided us with every good thing and that life's primary task is to receive this goodness with great joy. After all, the most appropriate response to a father's gift is use, enjoyment, and gratitude. Our bodies, nature, music, art, food, and human relationships reflect God's purpose, design, and goodness, and using these gifts as God intended and delighting in them is one way to honor and glorify him. Not only is true leisure a path

---

1. Wirzba, *Living the Sabbath*, 33.
2. Wirzba, *Living the Sabbath*, 52–63.
3. Schindler, "Person as Gift," 401–5.
4. Pieper, *Leisure*, 26–27.
5. Pieper, *Leisure*, 44–48.

to human flourishing, but it offers a powerful witness to the truth of God's abundant love and grace.

Despite leisure's inherent goodness, many people struggle to cease from work, and even their nonwork hours are characterized by busyness, distraction, and the pursuit of superficial pleasure. For this reason, Christians must be disciplined and intentional about practicing true leisure and learning to rest in God. Leisure is more than doing what we find enjoyable, but involves ceasing from endless striving in order to receive the goodness that already pervades the world and our lives. This perspective on leisure need not lead people to be overly scrupulous, but should cause them to examine where their souls seek rest. Does our lifestyle allow us to marvel at the depth, wonder, and glory of everything in creation, enabling us to offer it back to God in the form of gratitude, worship, and love? How do modern social structure and culture influence people's ability to seek true rest?

Working Outside of Work: On *The Labor of Leisure*

In many ways modern social and economic conditions have made it increasingly difficult to practice true leisure. In 2010 middle-class married couples with children worked 577 more hours per year on average than they did in 1979.[6] Even beyond work, there are more things competing for people's time and attention in modern life. Commute times have increased,[7] Americans own and maintain larger homes[8] and devote more time to childcare[9]—despite having fewer children. Technology enables multitasking, but ironically makes us less efficient,[10] which exacerbates people's sense of busyness.[11] Many Americans struggle to cease working—even when given the opportunity—as they only use about half of their yearly vacation time.[12] Even when people do carve out space away from paid work, they often carry a mentality of productivity and achievement into their nonwork life. When people imagine their self-worth in terms of productivity, a mentality of work begins to colonize other areas of life (see chapter 3). In some

---

6. Mishel et al., *State of Working America*, 56.
7. Saldivia, "Stuck in Traffic?," para. 2.
8. U.S. Census Bureau, "Average Square Feet," see table.
9. Pew Research Center, "Modern Parenthood," see table.
10. Smith, "Multitasking Undermines Our Efficiency."
11. *Economist*, "Why Is Everyone So Busy?," para. 2.
12. Leonhardt, "Vacation Days," para. 4.

families, this involves devoting considerable time to kids' sports. Others turn home renovation and "do-it-yourself" projects into an ongoing mission to transform their homes through the methods and inspiration of HGTV, which has become one of the ten most watched cable networks in the United States.[13]

The sociologist Chris Rojek argues that leisure has become a form of labor, where qualities such as competence, relevance, and credibility are now expected across all domains of life—and must therefore be cultivated outside of work.[14] Many people busy themselves outside of work in an effort to transform their bodies and homes, or to gain skills and experiences that reflect their competence. People may experience a sense of accomplishment as they work toward self-improvement, but this ceaseless striving is not true leisure, even if it is people's preferred use of their free time, because its underlying motivation is instrumental, rather than to receive and enjoy the world for its own sake. This is not to say that people should not seek self-improvement outside of work, but a life dominated by instrumental activity stifles true leisure.[15]

Even seasonal celebrations have become colonized by this mentality of work and productivity, rather than serving as opportunities to remember and celebrate important days in the life of the church and nation. Our lives, and especially the liturgical year, are marked by rhythms of feasting and fasting. But holidays such Thanksgiving, Christmas, and St. Patrick's Day have become defined by busyness and excess—granting people an excuse to overindulge in food, alcohol, and shopping. Even those with good intentions may find it difficult to celebrate in the true spirit of these holidays.

Corporations perpetuate this problem by co-opting the deeper spiritual meaning of these holidays for the purpose of increasing sales. People are encouraged to treat these holidays as an opportunity to throw parties or decorate their homes, rather than being a time of spiritual preparation. Stores further distract from the necessary spiritual preparation of Christmas and Easter by peddling kitsch for months in advance. For Christians, the arrival of Christmas Day or Easter Sunday only marks the beginning of

13. Katz, "Most-Watched Cable Networks," para. 9.

14. Rojek, *Labour of Leisure*, 2–6.

15. Whether an activity is true leisure depends in part on its underlying motivation. For example, an avid hiker might be motivated by the pure enjoyment of nature and exertion of their physical body, which aligns with true leisure, while another hiker might treat hiking instrumentally—as a means to impress their friends, lose weight, or post pictures on Instagram—meaning it is no longer leisurely in the deepest sense of the word.

the season of celebration, yet stores quickly remove their seasonal displays to gain a head start on selling items related to the next season or holiday.

Corporations have even created new "holy days" devoted to mammon, such as Cyber Monday, "Spring Black Friday," and Amazon Prime Day. Days such as Black Friday are parasitic anti-holidays, which undermine the deeper meaning of holidays such as Thanksgiving: "Only in America do people trample others for sales exactly one day after being thankful for what they already have."[16] True celebration should be distinguished from "ordinary time" by feasting on good food and giving gifts, but our culture normalizes gluttony, overindulgence, and consumerism by passing it off as celebration. These holidays function as an invitation for people to celebrate their own desires, rendering them less able to truly rest in God's goodness.

Novelty, Diversions, and the Society of Spectacle

These misguided approaches to leisure and celebration are draining rather than life-giving. When people finally cease from work and self-improvement they are likely to be exhausted, which increases the likelihood they will seek rest in passive forms of entertainment. Many people envision free time as a reward for hard work, where they seek freedom and escape.[17] Often this involves turning to mindless entertainment, which is perpetually available through various screens. In previous decades television was people's preferred screen of choice, and even now the average Americans watches two hours and forty-nine minutes of television per day—more than any other waking nonwork activity.[18] But the screen attached to the wall is no longer the most powerful screen in our lives. The television must wait to be summoned, while smart phones buzz, chirp, and whistle their way into people's attention. Not only do people stream television shows from their phones, but they are a gateway to endless pictures, videos, tweets, and posts. At the end of the day or week when people finally cease from paid work and self-improvement, they can treat themselves to an all-you-can-eat buffet of information and entertainment without needing to leave the couch.

Technology also tempts people with a new kind of break during the workday. Of course, people's daily routines naturally fall into a rhythm of work and rest. The Rule of St. Benedict is founded on this principle, as

16. Howell, "Black Friday Campaign," para. 12.
17. Rojek, *Labour of Leisure*, 1–2.
18. Bureau of Labor Statistics, "Detailed Primary Activities," see table.

each hour of the day is devoted to prayer, work, study, and rest. But today's worker is more likely to be found in an office building, rather than in the field or a shop. The modern office presents its own challenges, as workers are tempted to rest in the constant stream of novelty and entertainment available through the internet. An investigation found that the clothing store J. C. Penney's 4,800 white collar employees watched over 5 million YouTube videos over a one-month span, which is equivalent to more than 1,000 videos per employee per month.[19]

People's ability to instantly summon the internet is no longer limited to any specific time or place. One study found the average person checks their phone about eighty times per day, or roughly once every twelve minutes of waking time.[20] Smart phone use has become so pervasive it seems misleading to describe it as taking a break, since the average user spends three hours and nine minutes per day using apps on their smart phone or tablet.[21] The head coach of the NFL's Arizona Cardinals felt compelled to grant players regular cellphone breaks every twenty to thirty minutes when he noticed they were struggling to concentrate during team meetings.[22] Simple tasks like walking or driving have become opportunities to check notifications. It has become increasingly difficult to be attentive to one's own thoughts—and even physical surroundings—as demonstrated by the fact that distracted walking injuries have tripled.[23]

It might be tempting to think that the only problem is how much time people spend using smart phones, or that they choose shallow, mind-numbing content rather than something of enduring value. These are important challenges, but they cannot be solved merely through more willpower due to design of the devices and apps themselves. The entertainment industry is well aware that a constant stream of novelty will capture people's attention. Scrolling updates, notifications, and flashy images mesmerize the human brain, because for much of human history such novelty was rare. Now the only barrier is our phone's lock screen. As people open their phones and swipe, their pupils dilate slightly, and a small amount of dopamine is released into the pleasure center of the brain. Dopamine rewards the brain

19. Madrigal, "How Much YouTube," para. 4.
20. SWNS, "Americans Check Their Phones," para. 2.
21. This is in addition to thirty-nine daily minutes of internet usage on computers. Nielsen, "Time Flies," see table.
22. Weinfuss, "Cardinals 'cellphone breaks,'" para. 4.
23. Nasar, "Pedestrian Injuries."

and motivates more of the same behavior, but too much can tinge activities with an addictive quality, as people experience the impulse to swipe and refresh at the first hint of boredom or loneliness.

Televisions and smart phones are not neutral devices that merely provide people with content they were already seeking.[24] Rather, teams of researchers at companies such as YouTube and Netflix study people's internet use and viewing habits to learn the secret of capturing their attention, intentionally designing products that nudge people toward greater consumption. Researchers have learned that people are drawn to shallow, attention-grabbing novelty, which is offered through a steady supply of headlines, memes, and tweets. This results in a "race to the bottom," where news sites and platforms are incentivized to prioritize whatever content will yield the most clicks and views. When one show, song, or video finishes, another one that seems irresistible is cued to automatically begin seconds later. "Binge watching" has entered our vocabulary, as people succumb to the impulse to watch just one more show. Platforms such as Twitter, Facebook, and Netflix have profited greatly from exploiting this weakness in human psychology, while eroding people's ability to pay attention to what truly matters.

Strictly speaking, people have the freedom to choose where to direct their attention within this buffet of information, yet they struggle to devote their time and attention to anything else. Is this freedom? Constant exposure to novelty dulls people's senses toward areas of life that appear less novel. This quest for novelty characterizes a "society of spectacle," marked by the "decline of being into having, and having into merely appearing."[25] The concept of the "society of spectacle" was coined in the 1960s, but has only become a more accurate description of modern life since the advent of reality TV, social media, and memes. Superficial appearances have become exalted over substance, while personality and charm have displaced character.[26] Spectacle looms large in our media landscape, and it is increasingly difficult for people to avert their eyes.

Many turn to mind-numbing distractions in an attempt to cope with the emptiness and hopelessness of modern life. Blaise Pascal referred to these as "diversions," which serve to distract people from cultivating a deeper interior life. In today's world every curiosity can be satisfied with only a click, which leaves people less free to satisfy the deep spiritual hunger that

---

24. Postman, *Amusing Ourselves to Death*, 83–86.
25. Debord, *Society of the Spectacle*, article 17.
26. Cain, *Quiet*, 21.

defines human life. Karl Marx famously believed religion was the opiate of the masses because it dulled people's experience of reality. Yet in today's world it is not traditional forms of religion that dull people's senses, but the pursuit of spiritual satisfaction, community, and meaning through an endless stream of content.

As modern people leave religious faith behind their lives increasingly become governed by a self-focused quest for meaning.[27] Modern culture now serves a therapeutic function, offering ways to help people feel good about their lives.[28] The priest or pastor has been replaced by the therapist,[29] or even the daytime TV host. Celebrities such as Oprah Winfrey and Ellen DeGeneres act as the high priests of this new therapeutic culture, parading feel-good stories and pseudo-religious ideas to fill the void in people's lives. This new religion promises salvation from meaninglessness and boredom, but renders people less able to experience the reality of God's goodness and creation. Christians must resist adopting the shallow diversions of therapeutic culture, and instead pursue the genuine meaning, purpose, and delight that can only be found in true leisure.

The Spiritual Heart Disease of Acedia

Since therapeutic culture is unable to satisfy people's deep spiritual hunger it inevitably fosters a sense of boredom with everyday life. This boredom leads many to embark on a frenzied search for fulfillment in earthly things. Boredom and frenzy may seem contradictory, but both stem from a deeper sin that few people recognize: *acedia* or sloth. A common misconception is that sloth is only an extreme form of laziness, but its disorder goes much deeper. Aquinas offers a more precise description: "sadness about spiritual good."[30]

Sadness at divine goodness not only afflicts modern people in secular society, but was a primary concern of the early desert monks who devoted their lives to God through prayer. They referred to acedia as the "noonday devil," because the midpoint of the day was when they experienced the greatest temptation to abandon prayer to seek some diversion. When facing acedia they were exhorted to endure: "If you are hungry, eat; if you want to

---

27. Burton, *Strange Rites*, 13.
28. Rieff, *Triumph of the Therapeutic*, 14–15; Rieff, *Fellow Teachers*, 120.
29. MacIntyre, *After Virtue*, 30.
30. Nault, *Noonday Devil*, 57–58.

sleep, sleep; but do not leave your cell!"[31] Leaving one's cell—even if only to visit a neighbor—represented neglecting the spiritual good of prayer that was the foundation of their life. For these monks, acedia manifested itself as restlessness and boredom toward the spiritual goodness of prayer.

Ironically, acedia's spiritual lethargy is often accompanied by worldly busyness, which is a manifestation of the frenetic attempt to flee the apparent boredom of one's circumstances to find meaning and fulfillment elsewhere. God offers a truly abundant life within life's present circumstances, but far too often people experience the urge to flee to circumstances and experiences that seem more desirable. Some have argued that acedia—not pride—is the most characteristic sin of modern life.[32] Today's Christians do not face the challenge of staying in a cell all day, but can we even drive to the store without checking our phones? Modern people don't need to seek out distractions—they find us. It is difficult to even imagine people sitting in a waiting room without watching television or scrolling through their phones.

The fact that much of modern life is experienced as boredom to be destroyed by the "noise"[33] of television, the internet, and other diversions is a clear indicator of the depth of the sickness that afflicts our hearts and souls. In C. S. Lewis's *The Screwtape Letters*, the demon Screwtape tells his nephew, "We will make the whole universe a noise in the end. We have already made great strides in this direction as regards the Earth. The melodies and silences of Heaven will be shouted down in the end."[34] This noise that fills modern life deafens us to the word of God made manifest in the world.

The effects of these superficial distractions are not only spiritual and psychological, but may even be physiological. The human brain has plasticity, meaning its neural pathways are forged through use. Pornography has been shown to rewire the brain, which affects people's ability to experience sexual pleasure—even causing some to prefer the counterfeit to real sex.[35] Smart phones may have similar effect, as heavy use is associated with decreased levels of gray matter in the brain.[36] While the smart phone's ability to rewire people's brains and alter their behavior is important in itself, Christians should be even more concerned with how this constant stream

---

31. Nault, *Noonday Devil*, 57–58.
32. Reno, "Fighting the Noonday Devil," 32.
33. Sarah, *Power of Silence*, 21–25.
34. Lewis, *Screwtape Letters*, 120.
35. Park et al., "Pornography Causing Sexual Dysfunctions?," para. 8.
36. Dunckley, "Gray Matters," para. 3.

of novelty and diversion might "rewire" their souls. Acedia is more than a lack of spiritual motivation, but an affliction of the heart that leaves people less capable of desiring the spiritual goodness of life in Christ.

Yet people often fail to recognize the effects of such diversions because they are relatively harmless in small doses. In a way these superficial distractions are analogous to sugar. Sugar naturally occurs in whole foods such as fruits and vegetables, and has been an essential source of energy for humans throughout history. For this reason, humans have developed a taste for sugar, eating as much as possible when it was available. In the past, sugar was primarily available through whole foods (such as grapes or apples), meaning it was digested slowly and did not adversely affect people's health. Modern food processes, however, can abstract and refine sugar from whole foods, allowing it to be added to food and drink in excessive quantities. This added sugar is quickly absorbed by the body, which provides a quick burst of energy, but leaves people hungry since refined forms of sugar have been stripped of the fiber that enables the body to feel full. Sugar is a good gift from God, but excessive consumption leads to obesity and heart disease.[37]

In a similar way, a steady diet of superficial novelty is bad for people's spiritual health. Refined sugar and superficial entertainment may taste good at first, but they ultimately fail to satisfy people's deeper hunger. Just as a heavy diet of processed foods and sugar could cause someone to prefer junk food over real food, people's souls risk losing their taste for spiritual goodness (acedia) if they consume a steady diet of novelty. Many people direct their desires toward the cultural equivalent of sugar: catchy pop songs, viral videos, and memes. These may provide temporary satisfaction, but they quickly lose their initial allure. Fine food, good music, and art are ultimately more edifying, but people must also learn to appreciate and enjoy them. For this reason, people must discipline their lower desires in order to "taste and see that the Lord is good" (Ps 34:8).

The effects of acedia on people's appetite for God is illustrated by the fact that many experience church as boring. Some Christians respond to this complaint with a dose of guilt: church should not be boring, and if people only arrived earlier to prepare themselves for church they would have a better experience.[38] Many congregations have responded by designing their

---

37. The American Heart Association recommends no more than nine teaspoons of daily added sugar for men and six for women, yet the average American consumes over twenty-two teaspoons of added sugar per day. Johnson et al., "Dietary Sugars Intake."

38. Rodrigues, "Bored at Mass,?" para. 4.

church services and ministries in ways that match the short attention span and tastes of the average person. "Meeting people where there are" means accepting that the average Christian will be more likely to attend a congregation whose music, preaching, and liturgy suits their preferences.

Such approaches may be able to temporarily increase church attendance, but to what end? Ultimately this strategy is a cosmetic solution to the greater underlying illness of acedia. St. Theresa of Avila's eagerness to hear the gospel led her to experience homilies as enthralling, even when the preaching was bad.[39] A soul that is properly disposed will delight in God at church, no matter the quality of music or preaching. On the other hand, people afflicted by acedia find the goodness and beauty of higher things to be boring and uninspiring, meaning cosmetic changes and guilt-laden arguments will be unlikely to change their hearts. Of course, congregations should aspire to offer beautiful and rich liturgies, but the underlying issue is that many people's hearts and minds have been rewired toward novelty, diversion, and distraction. The result is that many Christians are poorly disposed for true worship, which is sadness at the spiritual good.

John Henry Newman went so far as to argue that heaven would not be enjoyable for someone whose life did not form them to love God. In his view, heaven and God's presence could even be experienced as agony for the person whose heart is comfortable resting in the world.[40] Newman claims such a person might cry out like the demons from the Gospel: "Leave me alone! What have we to do with thee?"[41] Newman reminds Christians that all are called to the wedding feast, but only those who are prepared—properly dressed with their oil ready—will be invited to enter. If Christians find themselves perpetually bored at church they may not like heaven. Not necessarily because of theological ignorance, or even because they didn't want to like heaven, but because their earthly lives led them to acquire a taste for things of the world, causing them to lose their appetite for true spiritual goodness.

Rediscovering Sabbath and Leisure

The church must recognize acedia for what it is: a warning sign that even its own members may be formed in ways that render them unable to receive

---

39. Teresa of Avila, *Saint Teresa of Avila*, 100.
40. Newman, "Sermon 1," para. 5.
41. Newman, "Sermon 1," para. 8.

God's abundant gifts—perhaps even salvation. For the salvation of the world, including its own members, the church must call people out of this secular formation and into a sacramental way of life where they learn to "taste and see that the Lord is good" (Ps 34:8).

One of the ways monks combatted acedia was through the practice of stability.[42] Stability is more than staying in the same place, but realizing that God calls people to holiness within specific circumstances, relationships, and places. In other words, Christians must avoid the temptation to flock to congregations that offer a quick and easy spirituality—one where the music, preaching, liturgy, and ministry have been reduced to a superficial level in an attempt to gain members. Rather, Christians must recognize the wisdom of rooting in a specific place, with specific people, allowing them to slowly cultivate a prayerful attentiveness to God and others that would not be possible if they continually flee to more desirable circumstances.[43]

Such stability also allows true community to develop, which is necessary for the practice of Sabbath and true leisure. Sabbath, leisure, and worship are inherently communal, and lose some of their formative power unless the community is committed to resisting the temptation of busyness and total work. Yet merely setting aside time for Sabbath is not enough to cultivate true leisure, since not all forms of rest are equal. Some of ways people choose to rest may even distract them from God's presence and the deeper goodness of creation. This may sound absurd to modern ears, since on the surface where people spend their free time seems to be only a matter of personal preference. True leisure, however, involves the practice of learning to rest in God's goodness, which prepares people for the eternal rest of heaven.

Christians may not have intentionally rejected Sabbath, but its practice has been neglected in modern life. This presents a real spiritual danger, because "to refuse the Sabbath is to close the world in upon ourselves, by making it yield to our (often self-serving) desires and designs, and to cut ourselves off from God's presence and purpose."[44] In other words, failing to celebrate the Sabbath represents a rejection of God by ignoring the fullness of his presence in creation and our lives. The tragedy is that God commands us to enjoy him for our own good. Sabbath teaches us to delight in God through his world, which is already brimming with goodness, grace,

---

42. Cassian, *Institutes*, 219–33.
43. Okholm, "Staying Put," 19–25.
44. Wirzba, *Living the Sabbath*, 34.

and mystery, inspiring within us awe, wonder, delight, and joy. In short, it calls us to worship. Neglecting Sabbath—even unintentionally—fosters acedia and thwarts people's ability to enter into true rest, both in this life and the life to come.

6

Counterfeit Virtue and Practical Atheism

THE PREVIOUS FOUR CHAPTERS have sought to demonstrate how practicing Christians might become increasingly secular through the practices of everyday life. These practices may seem to have relatively little influence on Christians who maintain their religious beliefs and church attendance, but they operate at a deeper level by shaping people's dispositions of mind and heart. These underlying dispositions are foundational to the Christian life, which is defined by true transformation, or *metanoia*. Jesus clearly states throughout the Gospels that this kind of inner transformation is ultimately more important than mere beliefs ("This people honor me with their lips, but their heart is far from me" [Matt 15:8]). We may even act righteously without transformation ("You have heard that it was said, 'You shall not commit adultery.' But I say to you . . ." [Matt 5:27–28]). Still most Christians tend to treat beliefs and activities as the defining features of Christianity, especially when assessing the secularity of modern culture and the secularization of the American population. Rates of church attendance and maintaining theological belief are indeed important, but this book aims to reveal how secularization is better understood as a weakening of the virtues and dispositions necessary to live the Christian life.

Everyday practices related to education, work, consumption, and leisure can be understood as secularizing when they foster dispositions that hinder people from fully embodying the Christian faith. Modern education provides students with the knowledge and skills to become productive workers who succeed in the modern economy, but by doing so it invites students to imagine that what is most real is only what can be seen, touched, and put to practical use in the economy. This hinders their ability to envision the wholeness of reality, causing them to lose awareness of God's presence in the world. By failing to see God's presence in the world, Christians become unable to love and glorify God within the small moments of everyday life. Even Christian schools may unintentionally perpetuate this mindset, rendering their students less capable of loving God in their lives.

The modern economy is founded upon and further perpetuates a misleading vision of what is truly valuable, training people to evaluate worth in terms of production, prices, and pay stubs. As a result, people become disposed toward treating creation, other people, and even themselves instrumentally. Even if Christians believe that creation and the human person are endowed with deeper meaning and purpose, they have become disposed toward envisioning them as mere commodities, which obscures their true worth. As noted earlier, modern people tend to "know the price of everything but the value of nothing."

There is no question these approaches to education and work have produced massive amounts of material wealth, but true wealth remains elusive. In such a world consumption becomes seen as the path to happiness. Modern life is saturated with false images of what it means to live well, which restricts people's ability to receive the true wealth that surrounds them—fostering dispositions of ingratitude. Modern consumerism portrays freedom as the ability to satisfy one's desires, meaning people are prone toward restlessness and perpetually seek relief through diversions from the emptiness of modern life. Everyday life is characterized by various forms of novelty that seem appealing on the surface but have become a source of "noise" that obscures the depths of reality. As a result, people may find church worship boring because they have developed a taste for superficial novelty.

In sum, modern everyday life initiates people into a way of life that hinders them from cultivating the necessary virtues and dispositions for living the Christian life. The risk is that even practicing Christians will become practical atheists: unable to live in a way that truly reflects God's goodness and presence.

Christian Resistance to Practical Atheism

This secularity may pervade modern culture and social practices, but does it necessarily have these effects on practicing Christians? Many Christians resist these secularizing forces by actively seeking to cultivate a lived faith. Does secular culture still undermine their efforts to live faithfully?

For many Christians, the life of faith begins and is sustained through conversion experiences and moments of revival—and rightfully so. These are necessary and good, but they primarily relate to unsettled or "extraordinary" moments in people's spiritual journey. If Christians develop a spirituality that is dependent on good intentions and moments of revival—without more mundane forms of faithfulness—then they will be susceptible to the secularizing influence of modern culture within everyday life.

Ongoing conversion and revival are certainly good, but insufficient for counteracting the enduring and pervasive influences of secularity and its sinful effects. This is the case because sin derives from more than individual choices made in isolation, but occurs within some social environment—what John Paul II describes as a "structure of sin." Referring to the structural side of sin may seem misleading or inaccurate. After all, only individuals can truly be responsible for sin. John Paul II acknowledges that all sin is rooted in people's personal decisions, but he notes how such sins "grow stronger, spread, and become the source of other sins, and so influence people's behavior."[1] In other words, the actions of individuals cause ripple effects throughout the world—not only interpersonally—but also by creating and reinforcing forms of social structure and culture that perpetuate sin. Sin not only separates individuals from God, but results in collective patterns of thinking and acting that channel people away from God's intentions for the world and human relationships.[2]

John Paul II describes how the culture of death "creat[es] and consolidat[es] actual "structures of sin" that go against life."[3] This is not only true of unjust laws or evil practices such as abortion or pornography. Everyday life itself has become governed by structures of sin that distance people from God by inviting them to adopt a way of life that obscures its deeper meaning and purpose. John Paul II acknowledged that this

---

1. John Paul II, *Sollicitudo Rei Socialis*, sec. 36.

2. Finn, "Sinful Structure," 139–42. Finn provides a good description and assessment of the concept of "sinful social structure."

3. John Paul II, *Evangelium Vitae*, sec. 24.

structural understanding of sin is "seldom applied to the situation of the contemporary world," but underscores its importance by claiming that "one cannot easily gain a profound understanding of the reality that confronts us unless we give a name to the root of the evils which afflict us."[4] Even though people may resist its influence, this structure of sin is pervasive, deeply interconnected, and mutually reinforcing, and therefore is likely to influence *some* area of people's lives.

Another reason this "structure of sin" is so influential is that its effects can be difficult to detect. It is nearly impossible to quantify the kinds of dispositions that comprise modern secularity. It is far easier to focus on the measurable declines of Christian belief, identity, and church attendance as the defining features of secularization. Some survey questions might hint at the presence of secular dispositions, such as the fact that 66 percent of evangelicals use Facebook every day, compared to only 32 percent who read the Bible.[5] Yet the problem with this evidence is that people might begin to envision these phenomena as the problem itself: If people are using their phones too often, encourage them to take a social media fast or engage with more uplifting content; if they are bored, find ways to make church more appealing. These efforts may be helpful, but the problem goes much deeper.

Many congregations and denominations latch onto superficial metrics such as church attendance, beliefs, and participation in ministries and programs to assess their own impact and the spiritual health of their members. We live in a world that strives to reduce everything to quantifiable metrics, which are useful when requesting funding, stirring up people's fears ("we're losing the youth!"), or touting a program's success. Yet this statistical way of thinking is unable to capture the vitality of faith or the threat of modern secularity.[6]

---

4. John Paul II, *Sollicitudo Rei Socialis*, sec. 36.

5. Earls, "Divisions in Your Church?," see chart.

6. Rather than assessing modern secularization through statistics and trends, this book has adopted a hermeneutical approach that "reads" the underlying form of culture in an effort to show how it disposes practicing Christians toward secular dispositions of mind and heart. This allows for a deeper assessment of the factors that shape the Christian life.

Counterfeit Virtue and Practical Atheism

Counterfeit Faith, Hope, and Love

Another reason practical atheism is difficult to detect is that many Christians seem to retain Christian faith, hope, and love. Of course, the Christian life will always be characterized by some internal contradiction—as we often commit sins we do not want to do (Rom 7:16–20), but modern life provides many opportunities to exchange the virtues of the Christian life with counterfeit versions. The philosopher Edward Feser asserts that the four cardinal virtues have been replaced by more subjective counterfeits: wisdom has been replaced with open-mindedness, courage with empathy, moderation with tolerance, and justice with fairness.[7] Each of these counterfeit virtues is only a shadow of its true version, thereby hindering the development of virtue within the soul.

In a similar way the theological virtues of faith, hope, and love risk being supplanted by various counterfeits. Faith is not merely believing in God's existence and divinity. If it were, even the devil would have faith. True faith assents to God's will in all things, which not only requires good intentions but the ability to envision God's presence and purpose for creation. Without this deeper vision of reality people are limited in their ability to assent to the fullness of God's presence and kingdom. Reducing assent to mere belief reflects a counterfeit version of faith that does not intentionally deny God's existence, but unintentionally denies his purpose and presence in the world. Even if people continue to believe God is fully present in creation, they may become incapable of envisioning the world as a cosmos imbued with God's goodness and purpose. This counterfeit faith is formed in a social context that obscures transcendence, while compartmentalizing people's beliefs about God and creation from everyday life. Failing to envision God's presence in creation may seem to be a relatively minor concern given the many challenges facing the church, but this "eclipse of the sense of God"[8] is the beginning of practical atheism.

Christians must also avoid replacing true Christian hope with the counterfeit hope of "optimism," which merely longs for more favorable circumstances.[9] Some Christians seem to hope that the church can simply weather the storm by fighting the encroaching secularism of society through politics and legal battles. Others long for a widespread religious

---

7. Feser, "Cardinal Virtues and Counterfeit Virtues," para. 6.
8. John Paul II, *Evangelium Vitae*, sec. 22
9. Benedict XVI, *Yes of Jesus Christ*, 39–68.

or political revival to change the trajectory of modern culture. Christians should certainly work for good in society, but these strategies assume that the primary threat of secular society is declines in power and numbers, leading to marginalization. But even if Christianity were to regain its former political standing and cultural acceptance, modern social practices may still undermine the gospel within everyday life.

True Christian hope is not diminished in the least by the present state of the world. Near the time of his death, the philosopher Dietrich von Hildebrand remarked, "The situation in the Church is so grave that only fools can be optimistic; but I have hope."[10] The church's hope is in the coming of God's kingdom, which is not dependent on gaining numbers or power. Adopting this mistaken vision of hope might cause the church to imagine itself as just another corporation or nonprofit, which tend to seek power and influence through numbers and dollars.

Joseph Ratzinger warned, "The Church must not put numbers in the foreground and lower spiritual standard of zeal for the development of its organizational structures."[11] God's kingdom will not be brought about by gaining respect, power, or increasing in number. Rather, the savior of the world was born in a stable in a small town. His disciples were fishermen and outcasts. Tax collectors and prostitutes were drawn to him, rather than the respected people of his time (Matt 21:31). His kingdom seemed to end with his death, but it was truly just beginning. Even the apostles struggled to receive this truth, as made evident by Peter's response when Jesus revealed he must go to Jerusalem to suffer and die. Peter hoped for the coming of God's kingdom, but could not envision how Jesus' triumph required the cross. For this rejection Jesus told him, "Get behind me, Satan!" (Matt 16:23). Peter's hope was contrary to the way that Christ brings about his kingdom: not through numbers, worldly power, or clever words (1 Cor 2:1–5), but through what might seem like weakness—self-sacrifice and death.

Today's Christians face the same temptation to seek salvation and security outside of the cross. Ratzinger warns about forgetting the centrality of the cross, saying, "If the Church were to accommodate herself to the world in any way that would entail a turning away from the cross, this would not lead to a renewal of the Church, but only to her death."[12] God's kingdom offers the only path to salvation and sanctification, which requires

---

10. Hildebrand, "Optimism Is Not Hope," 4.
11. Ratzinger, "Ecclesial Movements," 485.
12. Ratzinger, *Co-Workers of the Truth*, 167.

suffering and the cross—not only Christ's, but also our own (Rom 8:17). This hope will always be secure because nothing can limit the power of his cross or prevent us from sharing it in our daily lives. Yet many Christians struggle to envision this true Christian hope because they have learned to imagine the church through secular paradigms of progress and success.

Finally, today's Christians must avoid adopting a counterfeit love that is based more on emotions, rather than a gift of self. Modern culture trains people to be consumers who rely on their feelings and desires to guide decision-making, but those who internalize this disposition will be incapable of fulfilling the Great Commandment of loving God and neighbor (Matt 22:37–40). God's love is cruciform—most fully revealed in Christ and his death on the cross. This does not mean that emotions are unimportant, but individual Christians and congregations must avoid adopting forms of worship that are aimed toward producing an emotional experience (more in chapter 7), which facilitates a privatized and compartmentalized form of love, rather than one that is embodied and self-sacrificial.

Modern Culture as Diabolical

These counterfeit virtues are deceptive because belief, emotions, and optimism are not wrong in themselves, but they are poor substitutes for Christian faith, hope, and love. Modern culture diverts Christians from true faith, hope, and love, while initiating them into a way of life and that obscures God's presence and goodness. By doing so it separates people from the wholeness of reality, while offering counterfeit forms of virtue that grant assurance that they are living the Christian life. In this way, modern culture is diabolical in the root sense of the word, which means to scatter or divide.[13] The word *devil* shares a similar root, which is fitting since the work of the devil is best understood as diabolical: separating people from truth, reality, each other, and ultimately God.

Exalting career preparation in education and defining value in terms of productivity is not only misleading, but diabolical, since it "dis-integrates" people from the deeper meaning of reality. Consumerism is diabolical when it trains people to approach the world as mere commodities, and modern forms of rest are diabolical when they separate people from experiencing what is real by diverting them to shallow novelties. It may sound extreme to describe these phenomena as diabolical, but the devil's

13. Schindler, *Freedom from Reality*, 151–52.

temptations are often subtle, dismantling the truth piece by piece by diluting and distorting its fullness (e.g., "Did God say . . ." [Gen 3:1]; "If you are the Son of God, throw yourself down; for it is written . . ." [Matt 4:5]). C. S. Lewis warns, "Indeed the safest road to Hell is the gradual one—the gentle slope, soft underfoot, without sudden turnings, without milestones, without signposts."[14]

Failing to envision God's presence in creation may seem like a relatively minor issue given the many challenges facing the church, but it undermines people's ability to fully embody the Christian faith. John Paul II claims, "It is clear that the loss of contact with God's wise design is the deepest root of modern man's confusion."[15] The truth of reality cannot be compartmentalized into a material component—which is the domain of education and work—and an optional, private, spiritual component that is relegated to the weekend. To do so fosters an "eclipse of the sense of God," which reinforces practical atheism: "living as if God did not exist."[16]

Yet many Christians are oblivious to how they have internalized thoroughly secular dispositions because they draw a sharp distinction between the religious and secular—assuming that secularity primarily relates to overtly anti-religious aspects of culture and media. From this perspective, people's faith remains secure so long as they maintain religious belief and activity. The concept of practical atheism illustrates how even those who believe and practice the Christian faith may unwittingly be formed in secular dispositions rather than the virtues of the Christian life. This is the primary way modern secularity challenges the Christian faith.

As mentioned in the previous chapter, Christians who inhabit a thoroughly secular way of life are at risk of developing a kind of spiritual heart disease—an illness within the soul that has classically been understood as *acedia*: sadness at the spiritual good. Aquinas describes acedia as a sin against love.[17] Living in God's love is the key to communion with God and others, but acedia is a sort of inertia of the heart that prevents people from returning the gift of each moment back to God as an act of love and worship.[18] Left unchecked, it causes people to lose their hunger for God as their appetite becomes redirected toward earthly things.

14. Lewis, *Screwtape Letters*, 61.
15. John Paul II, *Evangelium Vitae*, sec. 22.
16. John Paul II, *Evangelium Vitae*, sec. 22.
17. DeYoung, "Demands of Love," 178.
18. DeYoung, "Demands of Love," 188–90.

This sadness at the spiritual good threatens souls by weakening their desire to be transformed by God's grace. Acedia "dislocates" us from reality and the world, leading to a sort of "spiritual depression."[19] Josef Pieper suggests the person who suffers from acedia does not "want to be as God wants him to be, and that ultimately means he does not wish to be what he really, fundamentally *is*."[20] Aquinas recognized that acedia afflicts those who already know God, but resist the high calling of those who live in God's love.[21] C. S. Lewis's *The Great Divorce* illustrates how people who believe in God may refuse his transformative grace and salvation. He tells the story of several people who are living in hell but have the opportunity to visit heaven.[22] These souls were allowed to stay in heaven, but nearly all chose to return to hell, including those who were practicing Christians on earth, because they stubbornly resisted God's transforming grace. While their decision is shocking, Lewis's story reveals the possible fate of those who have become saddened by the spiritual good of eternal life with God.

Conclusion

Counterfeit forms of faith, hope, and love have been a perennial threat throughout the history of the church. Nor is acedia unique to the modern era, though contemporary conditions do seem especially to foster its existence.[23] Christians who have unwittingly been initiated into counterfeit virtues—leading to practical atheism and acedia—may still choose God's saving grace, but modern secularity works to undermine their desire for God. Secular influence is not limited to atheist college professors, the entertainment industry, or anti-Christian peer influence, but shapes the lives of practicing Christians through seemingly harmless everyday social practices. Not only should the church encourage individual Christians to remain vigilant, but it must also criticize contemporary forms of secularity that quietly threaten to undermine the Christian life.

Practical atheism may not dismantle people's religious beliefs, but it does endow them with secular dispositions that undermine their ability to fully embody the Christian faith. This way of life effectively pushes God to

---

19. Nault, *Noonday Devil,* 109.
20. Pieper, *Leisure,* 44.
21. DeYoung, "Demands of Love," 177.
22. Lewis did not intend this as a literal portrayal of hell.
23. Reno, "Fighting the Noonday Devil," 32.

the margins of life. Christians may have good intentions—attending church on Sunday, avoiding explicit immorality, being active in their congregations—but such surface-level religiosity is not enough to overcome the secular dispositions of thought and action formed within daily life. *This* is the crisis facing Christians in the modern age. How should the church form its members to counteract the practical atheism of this secular age?

7

The Church's Response

THANKFULLY MODERN CULTURE IS not the only influence at work in people's lives, since the church aspires to be a "culture of life,"[1] discipling people into true faith, hope, and love. Yet congregations and Christian institutions may also be shaped by many of the dominant features of modern culture. James K. A. Smith asks, "If liturgy forms us to the image of Christ, then why are Christians so often conformed to the world?"[2] This chapter assesses the church's approach to evangelization and discipleship. Do congregations offer the kind of formation that could offset the secularizing effects of modern culture?

Efficiency, Technique, and Control: Tools of the Modern Church

Understanding how many Christians envision the mission of the church requires an awareness of the underlying principles that have come to govern nearly all institutions and organizations in today's world. The sociologist Max Weber describes how a shift from substantive rationality (which privileges some pre-established idea of what is good or valuable) to formal rationality (which approaches decision-making on the basis of means-end calculations that eventually become codified as policies, rules,

---

1. John Paul II, *Evangelium Vitae*, sec. 21.
2. Smith, *Awaiting the King*, 168.

and regulations) characterizes the modern era.[3] As organizations came to envision their work in terms of means-ends calculations, they began to exalt efficiency, calculability, predictability, and control.[4] This approach is manifested in the modern bureaucracy, which occurs when organizations rely almost exclusively on policies and procedures that privilege the most efficient and effective means to various ends.

As mentioned in chapter 3, formal rationality underlies modern industrialization and mass production, where every component of the production process is subject to intense scrutiny in order to increase efficiency and profit. The social theorist George Ritzer argues that McDonald's is innovative because it introduced the techniques of mass production to a new sphere of life: food production.[5] By doing so, McDonald's revealed how efficiency and control could become ends in themselves. In other words, people appreciate fast food not primarily for its taste, but because it is inexpensive, predictable, and readily available. The use of new technologies, data, improved policies and procedures, and best practices has led to increases in efficiency, which most people see as an unquestionable sign of progress. Many Christians are optimistic that these approaches would be equally beneficial to the church. Will innovations borrowed from the fields of technology, business, and communications better enable the church to spread the gospel and form its members?

On the surface it might seem like the techniques and approaches of the modern corporate world—with some modifications—can readily translate to the world of ministry. This idea is consistent with the assumption many Christians have toward education, work, and media: that the underlying *form* of these institutions and practices is relatively inconsequential, so long as the content itself is neutral toward Christianity. But the fact that culture is most powerfully transmitted when embedded within social practices, rather than its overt content, suggests Christians should not underestimate the importance of *form*. This is the case with fast food. Even beyond the *content* of the ingredients themselves, the practice of eating fast food reflects a certain *form*—eating on the go—which hinders people's ability to eat mindfully and enjoy their meal in the company of others.[6] For this rea-

3. Kalberg, "Types of Rationality," 1155–58.
4. Ritzer, *McDonaldization of Society*, 16–18.
5. Ritzer, *McDonaldization of Society*, 7–9.
6. Ritzer, *McDonaldization of Society*, 20–22. Ritzer points out that by exalting policy and efficiency modern bureaucracies inevitably, and ironically, become irrational as they

son, Christians must not assume that techniques and approaches (forms) that seem neutral on the surface can necessarily be applied to ministry in a morally neutral way. Rather, they must discern whether the most efficient techniques and methods of ministry truly form people in Christian life and practice, or whether they tacitly encourage habits and dispositions that are antithetical to the church's mission.

In recent years many Christian congregations have embraced innovative programs and techniques in an effort to more effectively evangelize the world and form their members. This chapter will assess these approaches, including the strategic use of quantitative metrics to foster church growth, reaching audiences through online platforms, and the church's reliance on prepackaged programming. Are these approaches to ministry consistent with the church's mission, or do they have unintended consequences that undermine the virtue of religion?

The Church Growth Movement

One approach that relies on innovative techniques to more effectively spread the gospel is the Church Growth Movement. The founder of the movement, Donald McGavran, was a missionary who sought to harness the power of social science research to improve international missions. The movement has since evolved and now employs the use of consultants, best practices, and marketing research to help pastors in the United States organize their congregations and ministries in ways that will appeal to more people. Numerical growth is one of the movement's primary goals,[7] which is achieved by intentionally developing homogenous congregations that allow people to attend church with others who look, think, and feel like they do. Segregating people on the basis of various demographic characteristics is seen as desirable because it allows pastors to offer approaches to ministry and worship that are tailored for the specific needs of different kinds of people.[8]

Many congregations pursue growth by seeking niche markets of possible congregants. One data management group, called Gloo, collects data through apps and tracking cookies, which it sells to congregations for the purpose of reaching people with custom advertising campaigns. Ten percent of churches in the United States receive data from Gloo, and the

---

privilege efficiency over other human goods which at times may be more desirable.

7. McGavran, *Understanding Church Growth*, 67.
8. Smith and Pattison, *Slow Church*, 47.

average client pays fifteen hundred dollars per year to gain access to data that allows them to advertise their ministries to people who are likely to be lonely, experiencing grief, or going through a possible divorce.[9]

In the book *Slow Church*, C. Christopher Smith and John Pattison criticize how congregations have given themselves over to "plug-and-play ministries, target marketing, celebrity pastors, tightly scripted worship performances, corporate branding, the substitution of nonhuman technology for human work, church growth formulas that can be applied without deference to local context," which entice pastors "with promises of miraculous results in just a few easy steps."[10] These methods of ministry may shock the sensibilities of some Christians, yet congregations defend them because they bring people in the door. This reveals how many congregations have embraced the principles of formal rationality by adopting innovative and efficient means of achieving the end of church growth by calculating the needs, preferences, and desires of current and potential congregants.

Even congregations that bristle at some of the more brazen techniques of church growth may find themselves borrowing from the movement's methods and unwittingly internalizing its mindset. The book *Rebuilt* tells how one Catholic parish reassessed its approach to ministry by "drawing on the wisdom gleaned from thriving mega-churches and innovative business leaders."[11] While their goals were to make the parish more welcoming by improving the "weekend experience," and to help existing parishioners become more engaged at Mass,[12] they found that some parishioners adopted a mentality of religious consumerism, which the parish criticized and tried to avoid by prioritizing discipleship.

Congregations may have good underlying intentions, but how does their reliance on the methods, strategies, and mentalities of the Church Growth Movement shape their vision of ministry? Tracking various metrics may seem like a relatively benign way to assess the success and potential of various ministries. Statistics and data may help inform decision-making in some circumstances, but one risk is that leaders will begin to conceive of their ministries in quantitative terms. Pastors may unwittingly begin to treat participation rates as an end in themselves, which incentivizes approaches and techniques that maximize participation.

9. Safdar, "Churches Target New Members," para. 8.
10. Smith and Pattison, *Slow Church*, 15.
11. From the book's description on the publisher's website.
12. White and Corcoran, *Rebuilt*, 93.

The Church's Response

Of course, participation is good and necessary, but it is not the ultimate goal of ministry. Even ministry leaders who know numbers are a poor measure of their congregation's vitality may be tempted to devote too much time and attention to increasing participation at the expense of focusing on deep and enduring formation. The problem is that more holistic approaches are inefficient and their effects are difficult to measure. Rather than offering in-depth formation, congregations may come to envision their role as maximizing participation, while assuming that spiritual growth will naturally occur within various programs. Novel and entertaining programs may be enticing, but will congregations and participants whose initial priority is satisfying religious preferences be able to transition into deeper forms of discipleship?

Charles Taylor introduced the concept of the "social imaginary" to describe people's vision of social reality that extends beyond their stated beliefs. People also have an "ecclesial imaginary," which describes how they imagine the role of the church in the Christian life. This imaginary goes deeper than people's stated beliefs and is shaped by the assumptions, practices, and liturgies of contemporary church congregations. Imagining ministry in terms of the techniques, topics, and programs that spark the highest participation rates indirectly encourages congregations to become religious producers who rely on slick marketing, branding, and various forms of religious novelty and entertainment. Despite their good intentions, congregations who adopt these methods are incentivized to see members and visitors as religious consumers. Outside of the pastor's office at Willow Creek Church is a poster that asks, "What is our business? Who is our customer? What does the customer consider value (sic)?"[13]

When a critical mass of congregations adopts this mentality it produces what social psychologists call a social dilemma, which is a situation where individuals choosing to act in their own best interest ends up leaving *everyone* worse off. When enough individual congregations seek growth by appealing to people's superficial preferences, then the population of churchgoing (and potential) Christians are encouraged to make decisions regarding church membership on the basis of superficial criteria and whims. When such people eventually join a congregation they will be more likely to treat their participation as religious consumption, rather than membership in the body of Christ. Even though this strategy may lead

---

13. Twitchell, *Shopping for God*, 254.

some congregations to grow, it has not brought more people into the church as a whole, but merely shuffled the membership of existing congregations.[14]

Modern people are already prone to experience the world as consumers who are presented with an array of options, identities, and styles which they should choose between on the basis of their own preferences. When congregations compete among themselves on the basis of satisfying people's preferences, they unintentionally habituate their own members to become religious consumers, which hinders congregations from acting as the body of Christ. Such preference-based Christianity is deeply antithetical to the life of faith, which calls people to deny themselves, take up their cross, and follow Christ. Congregations that overemphasize messages, events, and aesthetics that seek to "meet people where they are" face the temptation to downplay or ignore the most challenging and convicting aspects of Christianity—which are necessary for transformation and growth. If Christians develop an "ecclesial imaginary" that envisions their own congregation merely as one more religious "provider" in a culture that is already oversaturated with people and groups who are vying for their attention, what will happen if their preferences change or another congregation offers something more appealing? Is the benefit of directing a herd of people toward a congregation worth the spiritual cost of fostering religious consumerism?

Peter Kreeft reminds Christians, "Jesus commanded us . . . not to sell the Gospel, but to proclaim it."[15] Yet many congregations are enticed by the prospect of growth offered by business and marketing techniques. Pastors may be tempted to act like the CEO of their congregation, whose role involves carefully crafting a message (How many pop culture references and stories? Expository preaching?), aesthetic (stage lighting?), and style (How should the pastor dress?) to meet the preferences and expectations of the congregation. Is this where pastors should be directing their time, attention, and budgets? Even if congregations supplement seeker-friendly approaches with reminders that discipline, obedience, and suffering are central features of the Christian faith, the overall ecology of American Christianity nudges Christians toward following their preferences. Christian leaders may decry the relativism that saturates American culture and the lives of their members, but they must confront the fact that their own congregations may

---

14. Drane, *McDonaldization of the Church*, 45.
15. Kreeft, *Back to Virtue*, 89.

rely on strategies that foster the mindset of relativism by exalting people's individual choices and whims.

Reaching the "Nones" Online

Another strategy employed by many congregations and ministries is to leverage the internet and social media to reach more people with the gospel. This strategy seems especially important since nearly 30 percent of Americans claim to have no religion,[16] meaning the average person is less likely to encounter practicing Christians in everyday life. Bishop Robert Barron is a pioneer and proponent of online evangelization, claiming that to reach those with no religion, "The most important thing we can do is to develop a digital outreach."[17] This optimism toward the internet and social media assumes they are merely neutral channels of communication. After all, individual users create its content, meaning those with the right motives could use these platforms for good.

Social media is not a neutral space, however; instead, it commands and invites certain habits of attention, thought, and communication.[18] This is true for both those who create and those who consume its content. Those who create content enter a crowded space where everyone is vying for attention in the form of follows, likes, comments, and retweets. To enter this space is to play by its rules or risk being ignored. The medium of social media encourages people to carefully curate an online persona, disposing them toward posting content for the purpose of attracting attention. The gospel certainly merits attention, but the question is where the church should present its good news, and how. If online evangelists grant too much priority to capturing people's attention they risk adopting the values and logics of sales and show business—seeking attention for the sake of selling ideas and gaining influence.

Similarly, those who scroll through a "feed" embody the practices of a consumer: ignoring what fails to hold their attention, and lingering on what does, but always moving on to the next post. As a result, the medium encourages seekers to first engage with the church as consumers of the digital content it produces. Evangelists may hope that seekers will eventually

16. Smith, "Religiously Unaffiliated," para. 3.
17. Smith, "Bring 'Nones' to Christ," para. 9.
18. Postman, *Amusing Ourselves to Death*, 83–86. Neil Postman argues convincingly that the medium of television is not neutral. The same critique applies to social media.

transition to a deeper encounter with Christ through embodied practices, but the risk is that the habits and dispositions formed online may distort how both evangelists and seekers imagine their respective spiritualities. Christians who spend too much time in the ersatz world of social media may find themselves gravitating toward spectacle, animosity, and conspiracy, over thoughtful reflection and sincere communication. The medium of social media fosters breadth, but not depth, making true understanding difficult. Those who respond with sarcasm and scorn are sure to accrue more likes and followers. The average person is likely to be fascinated by the conflict and drama, becoming disposed toward this type of discourse themselves.

Online discourse among Christians has become so vitriolic that Bishop Barron posted a plea for civility, exhorting mercenaries of the "flame wars" to "cut it out!"[19] Hopefully individual users will follow his advice, but the irony is that this type of discourse is fostered by the medium itself. Politeness, nuance, and charitable interpretation become less likely in a place that limits words and rewards mockery. Social media is more like the spectacle of the Colosseum than the sincere inquiry of the Areopagus in Acts 17. Just because people have gathered does not mean it is worthwhile to be in front of the crowd.

Despite these risks, this strategy of online evangelism seems to be fruitful because people appear eager to engage in religious debate through comments on message boards. But the truth is that a relatively small percentage of Americans go online for the purpose of having serious conversations about religion, and many who do are intentionally antagonistic—their primary motivation to air grievances and pick fights with people who disagree. Online evangelists may imagine themselves as missionaries to the furthest corners of the internet, but will winning an argument ultimately win a soul?

While some people may choose their religious affiliation by assessing the logical coherence of competing belief systems, this is generally rare. Yet many evangelists seem to imagine that presenting compelling arguments in support of Christianity in digital spaces will bring people to faith. Most people today are highly skeptical of strong truth claims, tending toward a form of relativism that defines truth as whatever feels right based on individual experience.[20] Even many Christians tend toward relativism, as made evident by the fact that 47 percent of practicing Christians between the ages

---

19. CNA Staff, "Catholic Flame Wars," para. 1.
20. MacIntyre, *After Virtue*, 11–12.

of twenty and thirty-four believe it is wrong to evangelize.[21] Another survey revealed that even among teenagers who attend church once a week, 42 percent agreed with the statement, "There are no definite rights or wrongs for everybody."[22] Arguments from reason, Scripture, and doctrine may be meaningful to some, but in today's world people are likely to filter such arguments through the lens of their own feelings and experiences, which they treat as the final arbiter of truth. Christian apologists may argue that individual feelings should not be the standard of truth, but this *feels* wrong to those whose hearts and minds have been saturated with relativism. Merely exposing people to arguments that seem compelling in the eyes of apologists will be unlikely to lead them into the Christian faith.

Even if today's "digital natives" find Christianity intriguing, what is the likelihood that the seeds planted through online evangelization will eventually mature to bear fruit? Those who receive the seed of the gospel via the internet do so in online spaces that are weak approximations of true Christian life in community. Even at their best, these online networks of support are spread across the world and are comprised of people who may not even know each other's real names. Even if online seekers become convinced of the truth of Christianity, how likely are they to attend a local church congregation and become an active member? And even if they do, what kind of embodied Christian community awaits them? Will their intellectual conversions—forged through online discussion and debate—translate to a lived faith in the context of the typical church congregation?

This does happen occasionally, and Christians should pray more people begin the journey of faith through the encouragement of online evangelists. Some may indeed be called to devote their time and attention to online evangelism,[23] but the church should not imagine the internet and social media platforms as a primary means of evangelism and formation. Even John Henry Newman, who knew firsthand the importance of religious argument, doubted that apologetics could form people in the Christian faith, saying, "I have no intention whatever of denying the beauty and

---

21. Barna, "Evangelism Is Wrong," para. 4.

22. Weighted data analyzed from the 2005 National Study of Youth and Religion.

23. To be fair, there are spiritual seekers who will look online for information, inspiration, and support. The church should certainly have an online presence for such seekers, but "digital media" is not a silver bullet that will reverse declines in religious belief and practice.

the cogency of the argument which these books contain; but I question much, whether in matter of fact they make or keep men Christians."[24]

Revealing Beauty through Social Media?

Another use of social media is not merely to present the truth of the Christian faith, but to reveal its beauty. Bishop Barron believes evangelists should consider revealing the beauty of Christianity before introducing rational arguments for the truth of its theology.[25] People are motivated by what they find attractive, which is an especially useful evangelization strategy given the relativism and skepticism that pervade modern culture.[26] Bishop Barron's Word on Fire ministry published a blog post titled "Instagram as an Evangelizing Tool," which asks "can Instagram beauty save the unaffiliated world?"[27] The author's answer is a qualified "yes": Instagram can evangelize the "nones" when it portrays the beauty of people rallying together to support good causes and each other through life's challenges, which extends beyond the superficial "prettiness" often found on social media.

Such displays of charity are certainly beautiful, but should Christians look primarily to social media to reveal beauty? Scripture exhorts, "Always be prepared to make a defense to anyone who calls you to account for the hope that is in you" (1 Pet 3:15). In modern culture, our primary witness is whether our life is a joyful expression of the good news we have received. Social media platforms may communicate the beauty of our life's witness in limited ways, but the full power of the gospel in our lives cannot be transmitted via tweets, pictures, and updates. It is no secret that most people carefully curate what they post about themselves online,[28] meaning that social media platforms are already oversaturated with shallow images of success, happiness, and other content that is "instagrammable." Can social media do justice to the depth and beauty of joyfully living the Christian life, or will nonbelievers envision online evangelization as more posturing in the noisy and overcrowded world of social media?

Those who look to social media as the key to evangelizing the "nones" also face the temptation to repackage the Christian faith in a way that

24. Newman, "Sermon 5," para. 18.
25. This approach finds its roots in the theology of Hans Urs von Balthasar.
26. Barron, "Evangelizing Through Beauty."
27. Tramontin, "Instagram as Evangelizing Tool," para. 5.
28. Freitas, *Happiness Effect*, 15.

The Church's Response

receives the most likes and comments. Is this the evangelization the world needs? Social media is inherently superficial, disembodied, and ephemeral. By contrast, the power of the gospel in our lives is deep, embodied, and enduring. John Paul II says, "Not all are called to be artists in the specific sense of the term. Yet, as Genesis has it, all men and women are entrusted with the task of crafting their own life: in a certain sense, they are to make of it a work of art, a masterpiece."[29] Beautiful lives such as these are what attract people to the truth and goodness of the Christian faith. The poet James Matthew Wilson adds, "The artist is simply one who perceives the order embedded in and constituting reality and makes it visible in some striking, new, analogous way. The artist is a receptive medium for truth to speak again to us, in the world and of the world, in all its depth, form, and wisdom."[30] The truth of Christianity is most clearly revealed not through highly curated snapshots of life shared on social media, but by consistent and close interaction with the beautiful lives of saintly people, who themselves become a medium of truth.

The power of personal witness is supported by sociological research revealing that people who were in the process of becoming Catholic were likely to be "circumstantial converts," who made their decision through the encouragement of family members and co-workers, rather than through an "intellectual conversion."[31] This suggests people are most likely to receive and cultivate the seed of the gospel through the embodied witness of people they deeply know and trust. Of course, Christians should be ready to provide a rational defense of the faith when necessary. Nor is it wrong to share the gospel through social media, but the church must not envision social media as the primary means of evangelization. Social media may offer exposure to large audiences, but the biggest challenge facing the Christianity is not a lack of exposure—it is the absence of enduring formation. This crisis that 6.5 people leave the Catholic Church for each person who joins will not be solved merely through innovative techniques.[32] Before the shepherds go out to seek these lost sheep, perhaps they should consider repairing the hole in the fence that allowed the flock to wander off in the first place.

---

29. John Paul II, *Letter to Artists*, sec. 2.
30. Wilson, "The Law of Art," para. 10.
31. Yamane, *Becoming Catholic*, 51.
32. Pew Research Center, "America's Changing Religious Landscape," see table.

The Ministry-Industrial Complex

Understanding these declines in religious practice—along with the rise of practical atheism—requires a deeper look at how congregations conduct faith formation. Most churches offer plenty of opportunities to be involved, as the church bulletin and weekly announcements broadcast a variety of book studies, speakers, retreats, and various programs offered by the typical congregation. The most efficient way for congregations to bolster the faith of their members is by choosing from the full of menu programs and resources offered by Christian publishers. This arrangement between congregations and the Christian publishing industry represents what might be called the "Ministry-Industrial Complex": ministries have come to rely on prepackaged resources, while publishers have stepped in to provide resources for every kind of need, ministry, and demographic. As a result, both congregations and their members have come to envision faith formation as participating in branded programs and resources that are professionally designed for mass consumption.

The resources offered by Christian publishers aim to provide information or inspiration—in the form of studies or devotionals—related to several predictable areas: Christian living, relationships, leadership, Scripture and theology, or cultural issues. Many of the best-selling books include study guides that are meant to be used in small groups. Participants may find the information and inspiration offered by these resources helpful, but what is their potential to bear lasting fruit? Retreats, speakers, and books may temporarily motivate people to change their lives, but real transformation can only occur when people's habits change. Adopting new habits requires more than good intentions and strategies, but requires belonging to communities who support the social practices necessary for deep and enduring change.

Many retreats and programs recognize this fact, and therefore involve a small group format, which sometimes is meant to continue meeting after the formal programming concludes. One program that follows this model is Alpha, which is an eleven-week program that brings Christians and non-Christians together to share a meal, hear a talk related to the Christian faith, and engage in discussion. The purpose of the program is to "support the church with resources and tools that help create a space where people are excited to bring their friends for a conversation about Jesus."[33] While

---

33. Alpha International, "About Us," para. 5.

The Church's Response

such programs do have an initial life-changing effect on many, what happens after people complete the program? The Alpha program suggests that after people complete the program "they can run Alpha on behalf of the parish and in other contexts, such as with youth, students, and in prison. In order to keep the pipeline flowing, it is important that the Alpha team is continually refreshed by moving hosts and helpers to serve in other parish ministries after approximately 2–3 years. Alpha can then become a springboard to serve the wider mission of the church."[34]

This description of its mission reveals that Alpha's ultimate purpose is not formation, but to bring people into the church and inspire them toward future leadership and ministry participation. Of course, programs such as Alpha often serve as a gateway into small group engagement and daily practices that facilitate spiritual growth. It can foster small groups that offer the opportunity to meet with other Christians on a weekly basis for prayer, education, and support in living the Christian life. This is perhaps the best type of faith formation offered by congregations, but can any weekly ministry or meeting provide the kind of deep formation that could offset the deep secularizing influence of the social practices and institutions that govern everyday life? Programs such as Alpha are certainly beneficial and could serve as a springboard into the kinds of daily practices that shape people's hearts and minds, but congregations must recognize that such programs are unable to offer this deeper formation itself within weekly hour-long meetings.

Another goal of the Ministry-Industrial Complex is to provide a deeper understanding of Scripture and the doctrines of the Christian faith. On the surface, informing church members by teaching about theology and Scripture fills a major need in the life of the church, since it is well-documented that both Catholics and Protestants suffer from a lack of theological and scriptural knowledge: one in three Catholics do not know that the Catholic Church teaches that the bread and wine used at Communion become the body and blood of Christ,[35] while 78 percent of evangelicals mistakenly believe that "Jesus was the first and greatest being created by God the Father."[36] These shocking statistics may lead congregations to believe their most urgent need is a solid presentation and defense of Christian doctrine. One in three young adults who left the Catholic Church cited disagreement with its teachings, meaning some may view apologetics as

---

34. Alpha International, "Impact of Alpha in the Parish," para. 6.
35. Smith, "Eucharist Is Body," para. 2.
36. Weber, "Heresy About Jesus," para 7.

essential for keeping teens and young adults from leaving the Christian faith.[37]

Of course, the teaching of Christian doctrine is an essential component of Christian ministry. Nevertheless, congregations should not think that merely clarifying misconceptions about the Christian faith will keep young people from leaving, or that a rational defense of the faith will bring them back. Such a strategy assumes people choose their religion based on whether its doctrines logically fit together to explain the world. People may cite theological disagreement as motivating their decision to leave the church, but there is good reason to believe this is not the underlying cause. Such a decision is the culmination of a mixture of experiences, emotions, and reasoning. While many factors converge to influence whether young people remain Christian or leave the church, research suggests that parents are by far the most important factor—not because of their ability to teach doctrine, but because they are the ones who model the importance and (hopefully) attractiveness of centering one's life on the Christian faith.[38] This is made evident by the fact that people who become religious "nones" are very unlikely to come from devout families.[39] Religious "nones" are being honest when they report they no longer accept the vision of reality offered by Christianity, but this is most likely due to the fact that their hearts and minds were never properly formed in the first place.

Sociological research also suggests people are not neutral observers of their own religious conversion (or deconversion), but interpret it through the lens of their new religious outlook.[40] This means the "nones" are likely to draw on anti-Christian clichés to justify their position, such as the idea that religion and science are incompatible or that Christians necessarily hate people who are gay. Just because former Christians express strong disagreement with Christian doctrine after their disaffiliation does not necessarily mean these doctrinal disagreements *themselves* set them on the path to becoming a "none," nor will offering an airtight defense of Christian doctrine fix the underlying problem, which is their deficient formation.

While knowledge of Christian doctrine is a foundational component of the life of faith, sermons, classes, and moralizing are generally insufficient to generate spiritual transformation. Yet many ministries continue to

---

37. McCarty and Vitek, *Going, Going, Gone*, 24–27.
38. Bartkus and Smith, "Catholic Religious Parenting," 7.
39. Manglos-Weber and Smith, *Understanding Former Young Catholics*, 18.
40. Jindra, "Conversion Narratives," 289–90.

operate as if this were the case. When people become Catholic they begin a yearlong program called the Rite of Christian Initiation for Adults (RCIA), which involves attending weekly meetings that are centered on teaching doctrine. Though RCIA often involves some spiritual practices and the opportunity to attend a retreat, the vast majority of the process is devoted to lecture, discussion, and question and answer.[41] The leaders of RCIA would certainly state that Christian faith is more than an intellectual activity, but this process of becoming a full member of the church suggests otherwise.

Formation beyond Programming

Of course, programs such as Alpha or RCIA often have a positive influence in people's lives, but are they able to offset the secularizing effects of modern culture? This chapter's critique of the taken-for-granted strategies of contemporary congregations is not an argument for ignoring people's needs, or completely dismissing online platforms and prepackaged programs. Such strategies could offer some benefits, but only when they supplement a deeper and more formative approach to ministry. The problem is that the church has been too quick to adopt the techniques of business, marketing, and technology without properly discerning how these techniques might change people's understanding and practice of the Christian faith.

"Meeting people where they are" and designing church with an eye toward getting people in the door seems harmless enough, but this unintentionally perpetuates a kind of religious consumerism—even among church members whose participation would not otherwise be reliant on religious novelty. Such approaches also rely on a superficial understanding of cultural transmission and religious formation, while treating the Christian faith primarily as a matter of holding the right beliefs and being active in various church ministries. This has inadvertently led church members to imagine the Christian life as participating in programming that is characterized by passively receiving information and messaging, while those in ministry are tempted to see themselves as religious producers whose job is to choose and implement programs within their congregations. Programs may plant a seed or inform and inspire people, but true transformation is unlikely to occur without embodied practices such as prayer, study, service, and leisure that are practiced communally, and on a daily basis.

41. Yamane, *Becoming Catholic*, 103.

Practicing Christians, Practical Atheists

Joseph Ratzinger notes that sanctity requires more than participating in programs, claiming, "The saints were all people of imagination, not functionaries of apparatuses."[42] Therefore the ultimate mission of the church is to help facilitate the sanctification of people's minds, which requires more than drumming up program participation. Attending church on Sunday and participating in church programming may contribute to one's holiness, but do not define the Christian life. Church members may assent to doctrines of the Christian faith and be highly active in their congregations, yet have a shallow spirituality and relationship with God. Ratzinger warns, "There can be people who are engaged uninterruptedly in the activities of Church associations and yet are not Christians."[43] Religious activity may give the illusion of strong faith, but the low bar of program participation is not enough to foster a life of holiness.

True spiritual formation, like gardening, is a slow and labor-intensive process that may not seem very easy or economical for congregations. It is much easier to print brochures, offer inspiring music and speakers, and exhort people to try harder in their daily lives. Ratzinger suggests, "The Saints . . . reformed the Church in depth, not by working up plans for new structures, but by reforming themselves. What the Church needs in order to respond to the needs of man in every age is holiness, not management."[44] The church does not need an army of experts in event planning, marketing, communications, technology, and project management, but members whose lives are a joyful witness. Ultimately, seeker-friendly church services, online engagement, and informative and inspiring programming are incapable of offsetting the deep, pervasive, and embodied secular formation that governs everyday life in the modern age. Rather than fighting for minimal gains in religiosity by seeking new techniques, programs, and efficiencies, the church must ask what kind of formation is required for its members to develop the necessary virtues of the Christian life.

What Christians need most is not another book club, speaker, or even parish-centered discipleship group—even if they are informational and inspirational. Rather than aspiring to holiness for a few hours per week in a meeting room in the church basement, laypeople need to have their minds transformed by adopting social practices that foster sanctification within everyday life. For such transformation of mind to occur, the church must

---

42. Ratzinger and Messori, *Ratzinger Report*, 67.
43. Ratzinger, *Called to Communion*, 145.
44. Ratzinger, *Called to Communion*, 53.

be more than a weekly commitment or merely the authority behind some abstract beliefs that remain tucked away in the corners of people's minds. The Catholic novelist Flannery O'Connor once defended the real presence of the Eucharist by saying, "Well, if it's a symbol, to hell with it."[45] Perhaps Christians should have a similar attitude toward reducing the church to a provider of programming, sacrament dispensary, defender of orthodox theology, or center of social activism. If this is all the church is, then to hell with it. The church is not a club for Christians, but the bride of Christ, calling her members to full union with God through the transformation of their minds. How can the church bring about this conversion of heart and mind for its members living within modern secular culture?

---

45. Antonetti, "More Than a Symbol," para. 1.

---- 8 ----

The True Politics of the Church

THIS BOOK EXPLORES HOW modern secular culture shapes the lives of practicing Christians, arguing that culture's influence is not transmitted primarily through overt messaging (e.g., media), but rather is embedded within everyday social practices that lead people to internalize secular dispositions. Just as modern secularity is powerfully embedded and embodied, the life of the church has become increasingly disembedded and disembodied. Even though churches have been quite intentional about organizing their worship services and ministries to maximize their reach, these efforts have fostered an environment where congregations compete to offer increasingly sophisticated and enticing religious products, which encourages Christians to envision their church involvement as choosing between their available options for finding meaning, purpose, and support. This may seem like a positive development, but it ends up creating a marketplace where various producers (congregations) and consumers (individual Christians) make decisions based on maximizing participation rates or satisfying preferences.

Even though Christians' lived faith is prone toward being disembedded and disembodied, their lives must be embedded *somewhere*, enchanted by *some* vision of reality, and embodying *some* dispositions. By accepting a compartmentalized and disembedded role, the church grants other institutions and organizations too much formative influence over the lives of its members. By abdicating its formative role in favor of becoming a religious producer, the church has allowed institutions such as politics and the market to become the primary sources of enchantment in people's lives, which represents what William Cavanaugh calls a "migration of the holy."[1] For the church to offset the formative power of such institutions, it must rediscover a more embedded and embodied form of existence. In other words, the church must recover its proper political nature—understood as a body that shapes its members' lives in all areas, extending beyond Sunday morning.

The Church as Political

Calling for the church to embrace a political identity will raise many objections. Americans are quite unified around the idea that the separation of church and state is a good thing, and the folk wisdom that "politics and religion don't mix" is nearly unquestionable.[2] When Christians prioritize political ideology over theology, the result is often ugly. Yet suggesting that the church rediscover its political nature is by no means a call to import liberal or conservative policy positions into the church, or to grant the church control over the American political system.[3] Questions related to the possible faults of liberal democracy[4] or how Christians should navigate a two-party system are highly important, but the church's "politics" is first and foremost defined by more fundamental questions related to how it organizes itself as a community, the role it plays in the lives of its members, and how it relates to other formative polities, institutions, and associations.[5]

Recovering a broader understanding of the political nature of life is necessary to understand the church's "politics." Generally speaking, politics deals with how to govern or organize some community. This certainly includes the election of leaders, their exercise of power, and the kinds of laws and policies they enact to govern a particular community. Most people only think about politics at its highest level of organization: the modern nation-state. Yet people also belong to many intermediary communities and associations, such as families, neighborhoods, churches, voluntary

---

1. Cavanaugh, *Migration of the Holy*, 4.

2. Despite the fact that a small minority of scholars and journalists have called the separation of church and state into question.

3. The question of liberalism and integralism is an interesting one that goes beyond the scope of this book. The church may align with some liberal or conservative policy positions, but the point is that Christians should arrive at such positions on the basis of a Christian understanding of reality.

4. See Deneen, *Why Liberalism Failed*, 1–20.

5. This understanding is made possible by a broader understanding that politics relates to formation in community. See Smith, *Awaiting the King*, 9.

associations, and local forms of government. Each of these associations is also political because they govern people's lives, and often include political components such as leaders, power, and policies. Yet these lower-level political associations are more likely to be organized by concrete forms of culture (customs, norms, traditions, rituals) and social structure (routines, practices, etc.), rather than abstract policies that are implemented from the top down.[6]

Despite the fact that people often fail to recognize their formative power, the embodied practices related to these lower-level communities most directly shape people's everyday lives—often more so than the abstract policies of higher-level political bodies such as the nation-state. This is not to say that the laws and policies of the nation-state are unimportant, but their influence is less direct. The government can enact educational or economic policies that structure how lower-level organizations operate—even fostering approaches to learning, working, and consuming that are profoundly detrimental to human flourishing—but these policies only touch people's lives when embedded in practices at the local level, which are generally mediated through lower-level institutions. Individuals and groups who have awareness and intentionality retain the freedom and power to resist if they choose. Yet the decision to resist will likely be ineffective if undertaken by isolated individuals. Those who wish to live by a different set of values must come together and form their own communities and practices that will govern their lives by a different standard.

From this perspective, the church's primary task is to embrace its role as an "alternative political community,"[7] providing counter-formation that could offset the deformative influence of modern secular culture. The church accomplishes this task not by exercising coercive power, but through self-giving love. Without embracing its political nature as *this* kind of embodied community, the church will be unable to truly shape people's lives—whether those of its own members or non-Christians. This is the political vocation and nature of the church.

Despite the importance of this kind of politics, American Christians devote little attention to how their lives are governed by the culture and daily practices of lower level political communities such as the family, congregation, neighborhood, and city, yet they are overly eager to engage in political discourse related to national issues. Such issues are important, but

---

6. Though they are shaped by higher-level political authorities such as the nation-state.
7. Hauerwas, "Sectarian Temptation," 101.

an even more important question is how the church can avoid becoming disembedded and disembodied in a cultural landscape that invites it to accept a secondary role as a private purveyor of religious experience and meaning. The purpose of this chapter is to redirect attention toward this more fundamental aspect of politics: how should the church organize itself so that the self-giving love of the gospel is embedded and embodied within the everyday life of its members, who then bring it into the world?

The Church as a Body

Even though the church has a political nature, it is more than another voluntary association, interest group, or nongovernmental organization. The church is the body of Christ on earth, and therefore is endowed with a special identity and mission that is radically different from any other community or association. The church is "a chosen race, a royal priesthood, a holy nation, God's own people" (1 Pet 2:9), that "offer[s] spiritual sacrifices acceptable to God through Jesus Christ" (1 Pet 2:5). Offering spiritual sacrifices requires more than good intentions, but involves concrete actions within the circumstances of everyday life. The "liturgy" of our lives is "to do the world as the world was meant to be done."[8] By doing so, the church is able to both embody the Christian faith and embed its logic within all areas of life.

But the question remains, how exactly should Christians—and the church as a body—accomplish this task? Many rely on the notion that Christians should be "in but not of the world" as a guide for understanding this calling (John 17:15–18). Often this is interpreted to mean that the church must send its individual members into various spheres of influence, including law, education, politics, and business. Yet those whose lives are firmly planted in institutions that are governed by secular logics risk adopting and internalizing secular assumptions and dispositions, thereby becoming "of" the world. Given the possibility of this deformative influence, how should Christians successfully navigate being "in but not of the world"?

For many, the exhortation to be "in" the world is an affirmation that Christians should not separate themselves from non-Christians or withdraw from mainstream society. While most Christians would agree with this sentiment, the exact details of how they should relate to non-Christian institutions and social networks remains hazy. This question touches on

8. Fagerberg, *Consecrating the World*, see back cover.

such a wide variety of spheres of life and issues that the rallying cry to be "in" the world becomes meaningless without a more precise way of understanding how exactly Christians ought to accomplish this task.

James Davison Hunter's *To Change the World* offers a more specific answer by exhorting Christians to pursue "faithful presence," which allows them to seek the flourishing of others—both inside and outside the church[9]—by extending sacrificial love into the world.[10] Hunter details how Christians have mistakenly accommodated, withdrawn, or been overly combative toward "the world"—often seeking to exercise national political power in an attempt to resist secular influence. Hunter argues these efforts are doomed to fail because culture is controlled by elite institutions (e.g., media, higher education, and business) that are generally resistant to Christianity's ethos. Instead of striving to gain pockets of power in the hopes of changing culture (which will ultimately be ineffective), Hunter argues that Christians must seek faithful presence in all areas of life—not for the purpose of exercising coercive power—but in order to offset the dehumanizing tendencies of modern institutions by "creat[ing] space that fosters meaning, purpose, and belonging" and thereby "resist an instrumentalization endemic to the modern world that tends to reduce the value of people and the worth of creation to mere utility."[11]

Hunter's vision of faithful presence is a helpful starting point for thinking about how Christians should be "in" the world without compromising their faith or grasping for coercive power. But one question remains: do the church's methods of formation truly enable its members to embody faithful presence within institutions governed by a secular logic? Hunter acknowledges that Christians may face the temptation to obscure or downplay their Christian identity in public life.[12] For this reason, Christian engagement in public life requires "a critical assessment of the metaphysical, epistemological, and anthropological assumptions that undergird modern institutions."[13] Hunter believes this is a necessary first step for "the church

---

9. Hunter hopes faithful presence can help institutions to foster "meaning, purpose, truth, beauty, belonging, and fairness—not just for Christians but for everyone" *To Change the World*, 266.
10. Hunter, *To Change the World*, 244.
11. Hunter, *To Change the World*, 266.
12. Hunter, *To Change the World*, 258–60.
13. Hunter, *To Change the World*, 235–36.

and its people [to] stand in a position of critical resistance to late modernity and its dominant institutions."[14]

While Hunter acknowledges the importance of this formation, his argument is founded on the assumption that this sort of critical assessment and formation already exists to such a degree that enables Christians to be faithfully present—without compromising their faith—within institutions governed by secular logics. But we must ask ourselves, have American Christians demonstrated the ability to transform corporations, youth sports leagues, and public school settings, or has their participation caused them to adopt the underlying logics and dispositions that govern these institutions?

The evidence from previous chapters suggests that American Christians often participate in these institutions in ways that lead them to adopt secular dispositions—importing secular logics into their local congregations, families, and Christian schools. Christians may optimistically view these spheres of life as fields for evangelism, but far too often their approach to being "in" the world has led them to become "of" the world. As a result they are no longer "in" the world fully as Christians, but in a way that compartmentalizes the Christian faith to Sunday mornings, lunchtime Bible studies, or wishing people a blessed day. Without proper formation, even those Christians who desire "faithful presence" will be incapable of participating in business, education, and media in a way that witnesses to a different vision of living a truly excellent life.

This does not mean that Christians should completely withdraw from these institutions, but the church must ensure that those who will be sent embody the virtues and dispositions of the Christian life more than superficially. In the United States, it seems to be the exception more than the rule that congregations would offer this sort of formation. "Faithful presence" remains a worthwhile ideal, but making its vision a reality requires more than simply exhorting Christians to be present in every area of society, even if they avoid the temptation to seek coercive power or influence for its own sake.

Forming Martyrs

Clarifying the process of formation also requires a more specific vision of the church's mission within the world. Hunter rightly notes that faithful presence involves sacrificial love, but how can congregations and other Christian institutions truly form their members in this kind of love?

14. Hunter, *To Change the World*, 235.

Practicing Christians, Practical Atheists

Without a proper understanding of embodying Christ's love in the world, Christians may reduce love to little more than volunteering in their local community and wishing others well. True Christian love certainly includes these aspects, but at a deeper level it must be cruciform—reflecting the image of Christ crucified. Cruciform love also highlights how the church's love is not only for its own sake, but also for the world, which implies the church cannot be *in* the world properly unless it is *for* the world.[15] Self-sacrificial love is never abstract, but occurs in and through the concrete relationships of daily life.[16] Pope Benedict XVI notes, "Even the 'yes' to love is a source of suffering, because love always requires expropriations of my 'I,' in which I allow myself to be pruned and wounded. Love simply cannot exist without this painful renunciation of myself, for otherwise it becomes pure selfishness and thereby ceases to be love."[17]

The problem is that modern life seems to encourage shallow forms of relationship where people can easily leave communities, congregations, or relationships whenever they become difficult or no longer fit one's preferences. Taking the path of least resistance undermines the stability and rootedness required for self-sacrificial love. When Jesus told his disciples that he must go to Jerusalem to suffer and die, Peter rebuked him ("God forbid, Lord! This shall never happen to you!" [Matt 16:22]) because *this* kingdom was not what he envisioned. Similarly, the thought of embracing our crosses might cause us to recoil, but this is the only true path to discipleship: "If any man would come after me, let him deny himself and take up his cross and follow me" (Matt 16:24). Jesus responded to Peter's rebuke by saying, "Get behind me, Satan!" (Matt 16:23), indicating that self-sacrificial love requires the cross: both Christ's and ours. There is no other way.

What does it mean for the church to take up its cross? The church's mission is inseparable from self-sacrificial love, which manifests itself in some form of martyrdom, whether the "red" martyrdom of death by persecution or the "white" martyrdom of dying to self through daily life.[18] This may be unsettling, but the lives of the saints reveal how a life that aspires to be a total gift of self—whether red or white martyrdom—can be joyful. Throughout history the church has taken up its cross through persecution,

---

15. Smith, *Awaiting the King*, 57–59.

16. Cavanaugh, *Torture and Eucharist*, 183. William Cavanaugh claims this is the proper understanding of Aquinas's view of charity.

17. Benedict XVI, *Spe Salvi*, sec. 38.

18. Kosloski, "3 Types of Martyrdom," para. 5.

The True Politics of the Church

suffering, and even martyrdom, but for Christians in the United States "martyrdom" is more likely to involve crucifying our selfish desires and embracing radical love within more mundane circumstances. When Christians and non-Christians alike witness such love they are confronted with something that is truly beautiful: the kind of love by which the world will know that we are Christ's disciples (John 13:35).

How Christians should witness to this love in public life is not immediately clear. This kind of love does not seem to have much place within day-to-day activities that define business, law, education, and media. Does this mean Christians should become martyrs by quitting their jobs? By no means—but this does challenge Christians to envision their engagement with the world as surpassing what is possible merely through the good intentions of Christians whose lives are centered in such institutions and spaces. Individual Christians may still accept the mission of resisting the underlying logics of efficiency and utility that govern such institutions. Yet the church must recognize that this is not the only—or even primary—way that it is "in the world," since individuals are limited in their ability to witness to the truth and enact change within institutions that are governed by secular logics.

Rather than being "in the world" as individuals, the church must come to understand its mission to be "in the world" as a corporate calling for the church to act as a body. Of course, individuals should not be discouraged from witnessing to the truth within institutions governed by secular logics. But the point is that individual Christians who are immersed in secular institutions are quite limited in their possible impact, while taking the risk that they would adopt the dispositions and assumptions of secular institutions and social networks. Instead of imagining their witness in individualistic terms, Christians must come to envision the church—acting as a body—as the central site of their formation and witness.

To some Christians this proposal may seem too inward focused. This may be due in part to the fact that some Christians view secular institutions and spaces as necessary for gaining exposure to non-Christians who need to be evangelized. Such evangelism tends to package the good news of the gospel in a way that forces people to make a decision regarding whether to accept various beliefs and living by a certain morality. Calling people to "repent, and believe in the Gospel" (Mark 1:15) is essential, but at what stage in the process of evangelism? Leading with a call to repentance seems to be less helpful in a world where many people no longer believe in absolute truth and are likely to experience the Christian message as restrictive, judgmental, and manipulative.

What is needed instead is the witness of living joyfully as one journeys toward holiness, despite life's inevitable challenges and hardships. Such a living witness cannot be relayed in a short conversation, nor can it be chosen through a few words—no matter how heartfelt. Rather, it requires embodied formation through daily spiritual practices. In recent years, many Christians have rediscovered the power of spiritual practices through authors such as Dallas Willard and Richard Foster.[19] While this recovery of practices such as meditation, solitude, and fasting is certainly important, to have an enduring effect they must become more than mere additions to individuals' spiritual repertoire, but must become pillars of the church's life together through communal, daily practice. The church needs to go beyond weekly programming and encouragement in individual practices by inviting people to journey together toward some good end. Does the church offer its members this kind of spiritual life?

Intentional Community, Intentional Institutions, and the Benedict Option

Community and formation may sound good in theory, but how should they be put into practice? For many, the idea of forming communities to withstand the forces of secularism will immediately call to mind Rod Dreher's proposal for the "Benedict Option." Dreher explicitly claims that his book does not advocate for complete disengagement from the world, but instead proposes a "strategic withdrawal of Christians from the mainstream of American popular culture, for the sake of shoring up our understanding of what the church is."[20] Nevertheless, Dreher is frequently criticized as advocating for separation from the world.

This common misinterpretation is perhaps due to the way Dreher frames the challenges of the modern era. From his perspective, the primary challenge facing Christians is the activities of secular and progressive groups who seek to undermine the church.[21] Dreher's writing (especially

---

19. See Willard, *Spirit of the Disciplines* 1–10; Foster, *Celebration of Discipline*, 1–12.

20. Dreher, "Accidental Benedict Option," para. 6.

21. Both Dreher's book *The Benedict Option* and his popular blog at *The American Conservative* frequently share extreme examples of progressive politics and anti-Christian sentiment to be found within culture.

his blogging) highlights many troubling trends within modern culture and institutions, but bringing these shocking examples into the foreground of his cultural criticism lends itself to interpreting the Benedict Option as a conservative reaction to various cultural and political phenomena, rather than a call to Christian formation for the sake of clarifying and strengthening the mission of the church itself. Of course, cultural phenomena and Christian formation cannot be neatly separated, but the attention and framing given to culture war issues lends itself to this interpretation of his work.

Another issue with Dreher's repeated criticism of the work of secular and progressive institutions and groups is that it could lead Christians to envision these groups primarily as enemies to be resisted, rather than people to be loved. In other words, Dreher's posture toward being "in but not of" the world does not seem to help Christians envision their task as being "for" the world. The gospel calls Christians to be "for" the world, including those who may hate Christianity and seek to undermine it.[22] Dreher and others who envision the challenges facing the church in terms of culture war issues may agree that the church ought to be "for" the world, but their approach encourages Christians to view those who oppose Christianity as enemies, rather than as people whom the church ought to embrace in self-sacrificial love, even at the cost of persecution.

This is not to suggest that persecution is desirable or good, but Christians must remember that it is a realistic outcome of embracing the church's mission to love others as Christ loved (Matt 5:11–12). From this perspective, the reason the church needs to devote greater emphasis to formation is not merely to oppose secular groups and cultural trends, but to form the kinds of Christians who embrace their enemies with Christian love, despite the cost. The greatest risk facing the church is not the opposition of its enemies,[23] but that the church would fail to respond in love.

Creating intentional communities and institutions that are truly "for" the world requires prioritizing the kinds of practices that form the church's members in the virtues and dispositions of the Christian life. Such institutions and practices should not exclude non-Christians, but must strive to adopt an inviting posture without compromising the church's essential beliefs and practices. Instead of trying to sell the gospel through more and

---

22. "You have heard that it was said, 'You shall love your neighbor and hate your enemy.' But I say to you, love your enemies and pray for those who persecute you, so that you may be sons of your Father who is in heaven" (Matt 5:43–45).

23. This is not meant to trivialize the religious persecution that exists in many parts of the world.

more sophisticated techniques, Christians must seek instead to reinvigorate the institutions of work, family, school, and congregation, which all too often privilege efficiency, technique, and productivity over the slow and unquantifiable process of formation.

Modern approaches to work offer income and career advancement in exchange for a growing proportion of one's time and attention. Work becomes the primary determinant of a family's daily and weekly schedule, place of residence, and lifestyle. As families grow accustomed to a certain lifestyle it becomes their goal to maintain and reproduce this lifestyle for children, often through elite schools and extracurricular opportunities. This meritocratic and consumerist approach to life easily becomes reinterpreted as the good life, especially when one's peers treat such accolades as essential to human flourishing. Families may experience themselves as having few alternatives when many in their social network affirm some variation of this vision of reality.

One way the church could respond as a political body is to promote businesses whose mission is not merely to make profit. One frequently cited example is the Mondragon Corporation in Spain, which is a cooperative enterprise structured for the benefit of workers and communities, rather than for the sole purpose of creating profit for investors. Mondragon was founded in 1956 and now includes over eighty thousand members across ninety-five cooperatives.[24] To foster solidarity among employees the average ratio of pay between the highest and lowest earners is five to one, and a portion of profits are pooled together to avoid laying off workers.[25]

This model does not ignore economic realities, but rather assesses the importance of various economic principles in the context of a larger moral framework that is beholden to a higher vision of what is truly good, while accounting for the specific needs of families and communities. Mondragon's model is not meant to be a prescription for all businesses or industries, but it does reveal an alternative approach that allows people to conceive of economic relationships as embedded within communities and existing for people's mutual benefit. Such an approach is more compatible with the Christian faith's primacy of self-sacrificial love, and is consistent with a vision of the good life that privileges holiness, relationships, and enjoyment of things in themselves (contemplation) over achievement and consumption.

---

24. Mondragon Corporation, "About Us," para. 1–3.
25. Herrera, "Mondragon," 7.

Similarly, modern approaches to education are typically rooted in the pursuit of practical knowledge over wisdom, which unintentionally obscures the deeper meaning and purpose of reality. Another way that the church could be "in" and "for" the world is by fostering faith-based schools that are available to all members of the church, which exist first and foremost to support the mission of the church and the true flourishing of its members. One critique of Christian schools is that they are beholden to the standards of elite education—charging high tuition rates and prioritizing college placement while merely paying lip service to faith formation. If Christian schools were to prioritize Christian formation they might struggle to find a critical mass of students and parents who desire an education that is fully integrated with the Christian faith, while also being able to afford high tuition rates. For this reason Christian schools may find themselves torn between the competing goods of career preparation and faith formation—privileging the former in order to attract more students.

The Diocese of Wichita, Kansas has taken a radical approach to Catholic education, offering tuition-free education to children whose parents commit to tithing 10 percent of their income. This model is only sustainable because the diocese asks *all* members of parishes to tithe for this purpose, and not only families with school-aged children. The diocese views this approach as more than a funding model, but "a way of living the Christian life,"[26] which is a powerful statement that Christian education is not merely a private good for those who can afford it but essential for the life and future of each parish—and even the whole diocese. Involving the diocese, congregation, and other church members as stakeholders in Catholic education is an indicator these schools exist *for* the parish and the diocese, and therefore are more likely to provide a comprehensive Christian education, instead of merely setting students on a path to upward mobility while offering superficial faith formation.

Corporations such as Mondragon and schools such as those in the Diocese of Wichita model how Christians might create institutions that are founded on a different set of assumptions and values than those that govern most work and educational institutions. While these examples may be inspiring, such institutions remain rare, in part because they require the support of communities who share a common vision of faith and are committed to embodying it within the primary formative institutions of everyday life. In other words, such institutions are unlikely to develop in

26. Bootsma, "Wichita's 'Stewardship Model,'" para. 3.

isolation, but are most likely to flourish when they belong to a larger social ecology defined by a vision of faith that roots all of life in the gospel's vision of the good life.

For this reason, if Christians are to foster such deeper, formative institutions, they must relearn and recreate more intentional forms of community. In the past Christian community did not need to be so intentional because work, education, family, and faith were often naturally integrated due to geographic homogeneity, lack of mobility, and a slower pace of life. But in today's world people's lives are much more fragmented, as their time and attention are split between many varied institutions and communities.

Recent years have seen a resurgence of interest in more intentional forms of community, where a more embodied, daily practice of Christianity takes precedence over lifestyle and career advancement. Intentional communities are characterized by living in close proximity—at least within walking distance—as well as a sense of commitment and responsibility to the other members of the community.[27] Such commitment does not imply people can never leave, but it does call for a different posture toward life, mobility, and career advancement. Rather than fleeing from difficult relationships or chasing career success, members of intentional communities find their identity in relationships, community, and shared faith, and would even turn down opportunities to advance in their careers in order to preserve the deep roots of community.

Such an idea is foreign to most Americans, who conceive of the good life primarily in terms of career advancement, income, and lifestyle. This is not to say that Americans believe community and relationships are unimportant, but that many are willing to settle for whatever relationships and community are available in the space and time left over from their careers. On the other hand, members of intentional Christian communities prefer a simpler lifestyle, and are willing to accomplish less in their professional careers in order to prioritize the greater good of cultivating strong relationships, communities, and congregations.

Intentional communities take many forms, but one specific example that embodies these principles in a compelling and beautiful way is the Bruderhof Community, which was founded in Germany in 1920 by Eberhard Arnold but moved abroad due to rise of Nazism, and now has twenty-six communities in seven countries, including seventeen in the United

---

27. Davignon, "Finding Joy," para 7–8.

States.[28] While many members work off-site, the larger locations (which have several hundred members) operate their own businesses that employ others from the community. Working and living on the same site affords certain benefits: workers enjoy flexible hours and their supervisors discourage overtime, since it would infringe on their own well-being and the life of the community. One man summarized how the Bruderhof envision work by saying, "I wouldn't say I'm 'called' to the specific job I'm currently doing. Living in community with brothers and sisters, sharing all things, and serving one another—that's my calling . . . It doesn't matter so much what I'm doing, but what I'm doing it for."[29]

While prioritizing community certainly is limiting in some ways, it also offers certain benefits that would not otherwise be possible. Some of the larger community locations offer schools and healthcare on-site for their members, which provide a more personal and humanizing experience. One member—who also serves as the community's physician—claims she is able to offer more comprehensive healthcare due to the fact that she knows her patients personally, while being willing to go above and beyond by fighting insurance companies on her patients' behalf. Such care and support become possible when the relationship is not merely between a patient and provider, but between members of a community whose lives are lived for each other's well-being.

No Utopian Solution

Intentional Christian community may seem appealing on the surface, but members are quick to note these communities are not utopias.[30] People may be drawn to communal life for a variety of reasons, but without a realistic view of its possible benefits and inevitable difficulties, those who seek it are bound to end up frustrated. For some, intentional community is appealing precisely because it offers the opportunity to form Christian enclaves apart from the sinful world. While the impulse to avoid being compromised by secular culture is admirable, this desire itself is not enough to unite people into a community that can withstand the rigors of communal life. Similarly,

---

28. Stober, *Another Life Is Possible*, xvi–xvii.

29. Stober, *Another Life is Possible*, 32.

30. Alasdair MacIntyre notes, "The charge of utopianism is sometimes best understood more as a symptom of the condition of those who level it than an indictment of the projects against which it is directed." *Three Rival Versions*, 235.

many people have embarked on experiments in communal living on the basis of some shared interest, commitment, or idea—such as social justice, care for creation, or agrarianism—but these shared commitments are an insufficient foundation for true community because they will eventually be ravaged by the inevitable disagreements, internal politics, and selfishness that plague all human relationships. For these reasons, intentional community will always fail to provide the kind of belonging and support for which people yearn. Instead of offering an easy solution to loneliness and social fragmentation, intentional community is best understood as a site for dying to one's selfishness and embracing the slow and difficult path of growing in self-sacrificial love for others. Is that what people really want?

Another "community" where people enter with high expectations—before facing a call to die to their own selfishness—is marriage. The fact that nearly 50 percent of marriages end in divorce reveals the difficulty of self-denial and self-sacrificial love—even for those who share a home, finances, children, and physical attraction. Yet marriage is holy, blessed by God, and considered by many denominations as a means of receiving God's grace. The Great Commandment's exhortation to "love your neighbor" is no abstract invitation, but must begin with loving even just one person. Fyodor Dostoevsky notes, "One can love one's neighbors in the abstract, or even at a distance, but at close quarters it's almost impossible."[31] For those who can accept it, marriage is a kind of training ground for true love.

Community can be another training ground in true love, since the commandment to love one's neighbor also seems to apply (albeit differently) at higher levels of social organization. While the specifics of embodying Christ's love will vary across contexts, the basic form of love as embodied and self-sacrificial remains the same. Unfortunately, many Americans approach institutional and communal life on the basis of their own desires and whims, which inevitably leads to isolation and fragmentation. People's desire for authentic relationships will not be satisfied merely by developing better techniques for managing their loneliness and selfishness, but by embracing the kind of social infrastructure that offers people the opportunity to die to themselves, which is the only path to true life.

If Christians are to resist the secular logic of modern institutions and culture and its accompanying social fragmentation, a new approach to congregational life and community is needed—one that is founded on the kinds of daily practices that can form Christians in embodied dispositions

---

31. Dostoyevsky, *Brothers Karamazov*, 460.

to offset the secularizing tendencies of modern life. Yet the Christian life is not merely one of negation: Christians also need a deeper and more all-encompassing formation for the sake of being truly "for" the world. Such formation is not possible merely through weekly programs, heartfelt worship music, or inspirational sermons. Rather, the church needs to rediscover its political nature—an embedded and embodied faith that forms its members in the dispositions of Christian love and holiness through the practices of everyday life.

9

Epilogue

THE IDEAS IN THIS book are radical—and may seem unnecessary. After all, it is completely possible to maintain the status quo in one's career, while sending one's children to Christian schools, being involved in a good church, and developing supportive relationships. This may be the experience of many readers of this book, who have the determination to maintain a vibrant spiritual life despite the forces of secularity that pervade modern culture. Yet many others in our denominations, congregations, and families are experiencing dwindling religious vitality, in part because they have been thoroughly formed in secular dispositions. Even those Christians who are strong in their faith must question whether they would grow further in the Christian life if they lived within a social infrastructure that fostered daily, embodied formation. The costs of choosing such a radical life of faith are high, but if modern culture and institutions are truly embedded with a secular logic, then Christians must question how they will ensure the Christian faith is embedded and embodied in the lives of their families and communities in a way that surpasses a merely inspirational, informational, or therapeutic function.

There is no shortage of commentary on the ills of modern culture from a variety of academic and faith-based perspectives. Yet it is interesting how many of these perspectives arrive at the conclusion that a necessary component of the response to the challenges of the modern age is to recover a thicker form of community: Alasdair MacIntyre states, "What matters at this stage is the construction of local forms of community within

Epilogue

which civility and the intellectual and moral life can be sustained through the new dark ages which are already upon us," and that we are "doubtless waiting for a new St. Benedict,"[1] which Rod Dreher interprets in the form of the Benedict Option.[2] Patrick Deneen claims that we need a "counter-anticulture" that cultivates practices and not just better ideas about how to live.[3] Benedict XVI affirms the need for Christian communities that function as a "creative minority" in the midst of secular culture, publicly bearing witness to the gospel to both Christians and non-Christians.[4] David L. Schindler challenges us to see that community is not merely an "option," which implies that it is *extrinsic* to our nature as human beings, but rather that community is an *inherent* aspect of our nature since we always exist in relation to God and others.[5]

For many, the vocation of a thick communal life will seem too high of a cost, especially since it is possible to retain basic religiosity while maintaining the status quo of modern life. Yet the Christian life must be costly. Rather than trying to find the perfect balance of being wholly Christian without upsetting the status quo, Christians must be wary that the world—and perhaps even their own congregations—will exchange true Christianity for a version that allows for greater social acceptance and material benefits.

Christians of every age must pay some cost. What is the specific cost that today's Christians must be willing to pay if they are to embody the Christian faith in the modern age? Throughout history the cost of being a Christian was often martyrdom at the hands of those who lethally persecuted Christianity. In the United States few Christians will face this fate, yet all are called to martyrdom in another form: dying to their own desires and taking up the cross of loving their fellow Christians—and even enemies—within everyday life.

---

1. MacIntyre, *After Virtue*, 263.

2. MacIntyre rejects this application of *After Virtue*, because he sees *The Benedict Option* as calling for withdrawal rather than engagement. See Tradistae, "MacIntyre on the 'Benedict Option,'" para. 5.

3. Deneen, *Why Liberalism Failed*, 197–98.

4. Ratzinger and Pera, *Without Roots*, 120–21.

5. Schindler, "Toward a Culture of Life," 684–88.

Bibliography

Adler, Eric. *The Battle of the Classics: How a Nineteenth-Century Debate Can Save the Humanities Today*. New York: Oxford University Press, 2020.
Aladeojebi, Taiwo K. "Planned Obsolescence." *International Journal of Scientific & Engineering Research* 4, no. 6 (2013) 1504–8.
Alpha International. "About Us." https://alpha.org/about/.
———. "The Impact of Alpha in the Parish." https://alpha.org/catholic-context/impact/.
Andreassen, Cecilie S., et al. "The Bergen Shopping Addiction Scale: reliability and validity of a brief screening test." *Frontiers in Psychology* 6 (2015). https://www.frontiersin.org/articles/10.3389/fpsyg.2015.01374/full.
Antonetti, Sherry. "The Most Holy Eucharist Is More Than a Symbol." *National Catholic Register,* May 25, 2019. http://www.ncregister.com/blog/antonetti/the-most-holy-eucharist-is-more-than-a-symbol.
Aquinas, Thomas. *Summa Theologica*. Translated by the Fathers of the English Dominican Province. New York: Benziger Brothers, 1911–25.
Associated Press. "Farm Population Lowest Since 1850's." *The New York Times,* July 20, 1988. https://www.nytimes.com/1988/07/20/us/farm-population-lowest-since-1850-s.
Augustine. *Confessions*. Translated by Rex Warner. New York: Signet Classics, 1963.
Barna. "Almost Half of Practicing Christian Millennials Say Evangelism Is Wrong." February 5, 2019. https://www.barna.com/research/millennials-oppose-evangelism/.
Barron, Robert. "Bishop Barron on Evangelizing Through Beauty." February 19, 2013. YouTube video, 8:46. https://youtu.be/bBMOwZFpZX0.
Bartkus, Justin, and Christian Smith. "A Report on American Catholic Religious Parenting." Notre Dame: University of Notre Dame, 2014.
Bellezza, Silvia, et al. "Research: Why Americans Are So Impressed by Busyness." *Harvard Business Review,* December 15, 2016. https://hbr.org/2016/12/research-why-americans-are-so-impressed-by-busyness.
Benedict XVI. *Spe Salvi*. Encyclical Letter. Vatican website, November 30, 2007. https://www.vatican.va/content/benedict-xvi/en/encyclicals/documents/hf_ben-xvi_enc_20071130_spe-salvi.html.

Bibliography

———. *The Yes of Jesus Christ: Spiritual Exercises in Faith, Hope, and Love*. New York: Crossroad, 2005.

Berger, Peter L. *The Sacred Canopy: Elements of a Sociological Theory of Religion*. New York: Doubleday and Company, 1967.

———. "Secularism in Retreat." *The National Interest*, December 1, 1996. https://nationalinterest.org/article/secularism-in-retreat-336.

Berger, Peter L., Grace Davie, and Effie Fokas. *Religious America, Secular Europe? A Theme and Variations*. Burlington, VT: Ashgate, 2008.

Bergler, Thomas E. *The Juvenilization of American Christianity*. Grand Rapids: Eerdmans, 2012.

Berlin, Isaiah. "Two Concepts of Liberty." In *Four Essays on Liberty*, 118–72. London: Oxford University Press, 1969.

Bootsma, Caitlin. "Does Wichita's 'Stewardship Model' Really Work?" *The Pillar*, December 8, 2021. https://www.pillarcatholic.com/p/does-wichitas-stewardship-model-really.

Briel, Don J. "The University and the Church." *Logos* 18, no. 4 (2015) 15–31.

Brown, Callum G. "What Was the Religious Crisis of the 1960s?" *Journal of Religious History* 34, no. 4 (2010) 468–79.

Bureau of Labor Statistics. "Average hours per day spent in selected activities by employment status and sex." https://www.bls.gov/charts/american-time-use/activity-by-emp.htm.

———. "Time Spent in Detailed Primary Activities and Percent of the Civilian Population Engaging in Each Activity, Averages per Day by Sex, 2019 Annual Averages." 2019. https://www.bls.gov/tus/a1-2019.pdf.

Burton, Tara Isabella. *Strange Rites: New Religions for a Godless World*. New York: PublicAffairs, 2020.

Cain, Susan. *Quiet: The Power of Introverts in a World That Can't Stop Talking*. New York: Broadway, 2013.

Campbell, Colin. *The Romantic Ethic and the Spirit of Modern Consumerism*. Oxford: Blackwell, 1989.

Carson, D. A. *Christ and Culture Revisited*. Grand Rapids: Eerdmans, 2008.

Cascio, Wayne F. "The High Cost of Low Wages." *Harvard Business Review*, December 2006. https://hbr.org/2006/12/the-high-cost-of-low-wages.

Cassian, John. *The Institutes*. Translated by Boniface Ramsey. New York: Paulist, 2000.

Catechism of the Catholic Church. 2nd ed. Washington, DC: United States Catholic Conference, 2011. http://www.usccb.org/beliefs-and-teachings/what-webelieve/catechism/catechism-of-the-catholic-church/epub/index.cfm.

Cavanaugh, William T. *Being Consumed: Economics and Christian Desire*. Grand Rapids: Eerdmans, 2008.

———. *Migration of the Holy: God, State, and the Political Meaning of the Church*. Grand Rapids: Eerdmans, 2011.

———. *The Myth of Religious Violence: Secular Ideology and the Roots of Modern Conflict*. New York: Oxford University Press, 2009.

———. *Theopolitical Imagination: Christian Practices of Space and Time*. London: Bloomsbury T&T Clark, 2002.

———. *Torture and Eucharist: Theology, Politics, and the Body of Christ*. Malden, MA: Blackwell, 1998.

Center for Applied Research in the Apostolate. "Frequently Requested Church Statistics." Georgetown University. https://cara.georgetown.edu/frequently-requested-church-statistics/.

Bibliography

Centers for Disease Control and Prevention. "Obesity and Overweight." https://www.cdc.gov/nchs/fastats/obesity-overweight.htm.

Chen, Victor Tan. "Living in an Extreme Meritocracy Is Exhausting." *The Atlantic*, October 26, 2016. https://www.theatlantic.com/business/archive/2016/10/extreme-meritocracy/505358/.

CNA Staff. "Are Catholic Flame Wars Evangelizing Online? Bishop Barron Says 'No.'" *Catholic World Report*, July 8, 2020. https://www.catholicworldreport.com/2020/07/08/are-catholic-flame-wars-evangelizing-online-bishop-barron-says-no/.

Coleman, Rachel. "For the Sake of Knowing and Loving God." *Humanum: Issues in Family, Culture & Science* 4 (2015) 89–91.

Convey, John J. "Perceptions of Catholic Identity: Views of Catholic School Administrators and Teachers." *Journal of Catholic Education* 16, no. 1 (2012) 187–214.

Cross, Gary. *An All-Consuming Century: Why Commercialism Won in Modern America*. New York: Oxford University Press, 2000.

Crouch, Andy. *Culture Making: Recovering Our Creative Calling*. Downers Grove, IL: InterVarsity, 2008.

D'Antonio, William V., et al. "American Catholic Laity Poll, 2011." https://www.thearda.com/data-archive?fid=CATH2011.

Davignon, Phil. "Finding Joy in Intentional Community." *Front Porch Republic*, August 25, 2020. https://www.frontporchrepublic.com/2020/08/finding-joy-in-intentional-community/.

Debord, Guy. *The Society of the Spectacle*. Translated by Donald Nicholson-Smith. New York: Zone, 1994.

Deneen, Patrick J. *Why Liberalism Failed*. New Haven: Yale University Press, 2018.

Denman, Brett. "More Complicated Than New York City." *The Oregonian*, June 27, 2012. https://www.oregonlive.com/religion/2012/06/more_complicated_than_new_york.html.

Denton, Michael. *Nature's Destiny: How the Laws of Biology Reveal Purpose in the Universe*. New York: Free Press, 1998.

DeYoung, Rebecca Konyndyk. "Resistance to the Demands of Love: Aquinas on the Vice of Acedia." *The Thomist: A Speculative Quarterly Review* 68, no. 2 (2004) 173–204.

Dorning, Anne-Marie. "Consumer Reports: Two Thirds of Chickens Carry Bacteria. ABCNews November 30, 2009. https://abcnews.go.com/Health/consumer-reports-chicken-salmonella-campylobacter-bacteria/story?id=9210116.

Dostoyevsky, Fyodor. *The Brothers Karamazov*. Auckland, NZ: Floating, 2009.

Drane, John. *The McDonaldization of the Church: Consumer Culture and the Church's Future*. Macon, GA: Smyth and Helwys, 2001.

Dreher, Rod. "The Accidental Benedict Option." *The American Conservative* April 19, 2015. https://www.theamericanconservative.com/dreher/accidental-benedict-option/.

———. *The Benedict Option: A Strategy for Christians in a Post-Christian Nation*. New York: Sentinel, 2018.

———. *Live Not By Lies: A Manual for Christian Dissidents*. New York: Sentinel, 2020.

Dulles, Avery. "John Paul II as a Theologian of Culture." *Logos: A Journal of Catholic Thought and Culture* 1, no. 2 (1997) 19–33.

Dunckley, Victoria L. "Gray Matters: Too Much Screen Time Damages the Brain." *Psychology Today*, February 27, 2014. https://www.psychologytoday.com/us/blog/mental-wealth/201402/gray-matters-too-much-screen-time-damages-the-brain.

Bibliography

Earls, Aaron. "What's Fueling the Divisions in Your Church?" Lifeway Research, August 10, 2020. https://research.lifeway.com/2020/08/10/whats-fueling-the-divisions-in-your-church/.

Eberstadt, Mary. *How the West Really Lost God: A New Theory of Secularization*. West Conshohocken, PA: Templeton, 2013.

The Economist. "Why Is Everyone So Busy?" December 20, 2014. https://www.economist.com/christmas-specials/2014/12/20/why-is-everyone-so-busy.

Ehrenberg, Alain. *The Weariness of the Self: Diagnosing the History of Depression in the Contemporary Age*. Montreal: McGill-Queen's University Press, 2010.

Eisenstadt, S. N. "Multiple Modernities." *Daedalus* 129, no. 1 (2000) 1–29.

Esolen, Anthony. *Ten Ways to Destroy the Imagination of Your Child*. Wilmington, DE: Intercollegiate Studies Institute, 2013.

Fagerberg, David. *Consecrating the World: On Mundane Liturgical Theology*. Kettering, OH: Angelico, 2016.

Feser, Edward. "Cardinal Virtues and Counterfeit Virtues." *Edward Feser* (blog), November 23, 2012. http://edwardfeser.blogspot.com/2012/11/cardinal-virtues-and-counterfeit-virtues.html.

Finn, Daniel K. "What is a Sinful Structure?" *Theological Studies* 77, no. 1 (2016) 136–64.

Fortune. "Fortune 500." https://fortune.com/fortune500/search/?f500_profits=desc&mktval=desc.

Foster, Richard J. *Celebration of Discipline: The Path to Spiritual Growth*. New York: HarperCollins, 2018.

Freitas, Donna. *The Happiness Effect: How Social Media Is Driving a Generation to Appear Perfect at Any Cost*. New York: Oxford University Press, 2017.

Galbraith, John Kenneth. *The Affluent Society*. Boston: Houghton Mifflin Company, 1958.

Gay, Craig M. *Cash Values: Money and the Erosion of Meaning in Today's Society*. Grand Rapids: Eerdmans, 2004.

Glanzer, Perry L., and Nathan F. Alleman. *The Outrageous Idea of Christian Teaching*. New York: Oxford University Press, 2019.

Glanzer, Perry L., et al. *Restoring the Soul of the University*. Downers Grove, IL: InterVarsity Academic, 2017.

Gorski, Philip S., and Ates Altinordu. "After Secularization?" *Annual Review of Sociology* 34 (2008) 55–85.

GraphicSprings. "Most Powerful Logo Survey." https://www.graphicsprings.com/most-powerful-logos.

Greeley, Andrew. *The Catholic Imagination*. Berkeley: University of California Press, 2000.

Grim, Brian J., and Melissa E. Grim. "The Socio-Economic Contribution of Religion to American Society: An Empirical Analysis." *Interdisciplinary Journal of Research on Religion* 12, no. 3 (2016) 1–31.

Guttmann, A. "Statistics & Facts on the U.S. Advertising Industry." *Statista*, September 18, 2017. https://www.statista.com/topics/979/advertising-in-the-us/.

Gwynne, Peter. "How Much Is Your Customer's Time Worth?" *Kellogg Insight*, October 1, 2012. https://insight.kellogg.northwestern.edu/article/how_much_is_your_customers_time_worth.

Haidt, Jonathan. *The Happiness Hypothesis: Finding Modern Truth in Ancient Wisdom*. New York: Basic Books, 2006.

Bibliography

Hamlin, Alan, Casimir Barczyk, Greg Powell, and James Frost. "A Comparison of University Efforts to Contain Academic Dishonesty." *Journal of Legal, Ethical and Regulatory Issues* 16, no. 1 (2013) 35–46.

Hanby, Michael. "A More Perfect Absolutism." *First Things*, October 2016. https://www.firstthings.com/article/2016/10/a-more-perfect-absolutism.

Harnett, Sam. "Here's How Much You Are Worth to Facebook in Dollars and Cents." *KQED News*, April 11, 2018. https://www.kqed.org/news/11661387/heres-how-much-you-are-worth-to-facebook-in-dollars-and-cents.

Harvard GSAS Christian Community. "Shield and Veritas History." http://www.hcs.harvard.edu/~gsascf/shield-and-veritas-history/.

Hauerwas, Stanley. *In Good Company: The Church as Polis*. Kindle ed. Notre Dame: University of Notre Dame Press, 1995.

———. "Why the 'Sectarian Temptation Is a Misrepresentation: A Response to James Gustafson." In *The Hauerwas Reader*, edited by John Berkman and Michael G. Cartwright, 90–110. Durham, NC: Duke University Press, 2001.

Herrera, David. "Mondragon: A For-Profit Organization That Embodies Catholic social thought." *Entrepreneur*, 2004. http://staging.community-wealth.org/sites/clone.community-wealth.org/files/downloads/article-herrera.pdf.

Hildebrand, Alice von. "Optimism Is Not Hope." *The Rock*, November 1, 2004, 4.

Hochschild, Arlie Russell. *The Outsourced Self: What Happens When We Pay Others to Live Our Lives for Us*. New York: Picador, 2013.

Hollis, Nigel. "Why Good Advertising Works (Even When You Think It Doesn't)." *The Atlantic*, August 31, 2011. https://www.theatlantic.com/business/archive/2011/08/why-good-advertising-works-even-when-you-think-it-doesnt/244252/.

Howell, Park. "10 Brand Story Elements of REI's Disruptive #OptOutside Black Friday Campaign." *Business of Story* Accessed March 25, 2022. https://businessofstory.com/the-10-zbrand-story-elements-of-reis-disruptive-optoutside-black-friday-campaign/.

Hunter, James Davison. *To Change the World: The Irony, Tragedy, and Possibility of Christianity in the Late Modern World*. New York: Oxford University Press, 2010.

Hütter, Reinhard. "Why the Virtue of Religion is Indispensable for Attaining the Final End: A Re-lecture of Thomas Aquinas with an Eye to His Contemporary Relevance." *Nova Et Vetera, English Edition* 14, no. 1 (2016) 15–60.

Jackall, Robert. *Moral Mazes: The World of Corporate Managers*. New York: Oxford University Press, 1988.

Jindra, Ines W. "How Religious Content Matters in Conversion Narratives to Various Religious Groups." *Sociology of Religion* 72, no. 3 (2011) 275–302.

John Paul II. *Centesimus Annus*. Encyclical letter. Vatican website, May 1, 1991. https://www.vatican.va/content/john-paul-ii/en/encyclicals/documents/hf_jp-ii_enc_01051991_centesimus-annus.html.

———. *Dominum Et Vivifcantem*. Encyclical letter. Vatican website, May 18, 1986. https://www.vatican.va/content/john-paul-ii/en/encyclicals/documents/hf_jp-ii_enc_18051986_dominum-et-vivificantem.html.

———. *Evangelium Vitae*. Encyclical letter. Vatican website, March 25, 1995. https://www.vatican.va/content/john-paul-ii/en/encyclicals/documents/hf_jp-ii_enc_25031995_evangelium-vitae.html.

———. *Familiaris Consortio*. Apostolic exhortation. Vatican website, November 22, 1981. http://www.vatican.va/content/john-paul-ii/en/apost_exhortations/documents/hf_jp-ii_exh_19811122_familiaris-consortio.html.

Bibliography

———. *Homily*. Vatican website, July 22, 2002. https://www.vatican.va/content/john-paul-ii/en/homilies/2002/documents/hf_jp-ii_hom_20020728_xvii-wyd.html.

———. *Laborem Exercens*. Encyclical letter. Vatican website, September 14, 1981. https://www.vatican.va/content/john-paul-ii/en/encyclicals/documents/hf_jp-enc_14091981_laborem-exercens.html.

———. *Letter to Artists*. Encyclical letter. Vatican website, April 4, 1999. http://www.vatican.va/content/john-paul-ii/en/letters/1999/documents/hf_jp-ii_let_23041999_artists.html.

———. *Redemptoris Missio*. Encyclical letter. Vatican website, December 7, 1990. https://www.vatican.va/content/john-paul-ii/en/encyclicals/documents/hf_jp-ii_enc_07121990_redemptoris-missio.html.

———. *Sollicitudo Rei Socialis*. Encyclical Letter. Vatican website, December 30, 1987. https://www.vatican.va/content/john-paul-ii/en/encyclicals/documents/hf_jp-ii_enc_30121987_sollicitudo-rei-socialis.html.

Johnson, Rachel K., et al. "Dietary Sugars Intake and Cardiovascular Health: A Scientific Statement From the American Heart Association." *Circulation* 120, no. 11 (2009) 1011–20.

Johnson, Sheree. "New Research Sheds Light on Daily Ad Exposures." *SJ Insights*, September 29, 2014. https://sjinsights.net/2014/09/29/new-research-sheds-light-on-daily-ad-exposures/.

Jones, Jeffrey M. "U.S. Church Membership Down Sharply in Past Two Decades." *Gallup*, April 18, 2019. https://news.gallup.com/poll/248837/church-membership-down-sharply-past-two-decades.aspx.

Kalberg, Stephen. "Max Weber's Types of Rationality: Cornerstones for the Analysis of Rationalization Processes in History." *American Journal of Sociology* 85, no. 5 (1980) 1145–79.

Kaplan, Sarah. "Air pollution from farms leads to 17,900 U.S. deaths per year, study finds." *The Washington Post*, May 10, 2021. https://www.washingtonpost.com/climate-environment/2021/05/10/farm-pollution-deaths/.

Katz, A. J. "Here are the Most-Watched Cable Networks of May 2021." *TVNewser*, June 4, 2021. https://www.adweek.com/tvnewser/here-are-the-most-watched-cable-networks-for-may-2021/480168/.

Keim, Brandon. "Farmed Chickens Can't Walk; Just Grow Them in Vats Already." *WIRED*, February 6, 2008. https://www.wired.com/2008/02/chickens-cant-w/.

Kosloski, Philip. "3 Types of Martyrdom That Lead to a Heavenly Reward." *Aleteia*, October 31, 2017. https://aleteia.org/2017/10/31/3-types-of-martyrdom-that-lead-to-a-heavenly-reward/.

Kovacs, Gary. "Tracking Our Online Trackers." *TED*, May 17, 2012. Video, 6:23. https://www.ted.com/talks/gary_kovacs_tracking_our_online_trackers/transcript?language=en.

Kreeft, Peter. *Back to Virtue: Traditional Moral Wisdom for Modern Moral Confusion*. San Francisco: Ignatius, 1992.

Kwasniewski, Peter. *Noble Beauty, Transcendent Holiness: Why the Modern Age Needs the Mass of Ages*. Kettering, OH: Angelico, 2017.

———. *Reclaiming Our Roman Catholic Birthright: The Genius and Timeliness of the Traditional Latin Mass*. Brooklyn: Angelico, 2020.

Lamont, Michèle. *Money, Morals, and Manners: The Culture of the French and the American Upper-Middle Class*. Chicago: University of Chicago Press, 1992.

Bibliography

Lane, Robert Edwards. *The Loss of Happiness in Market Democracies*. New Haven: Yale University Press, 2000.

Larson, Erik. *The Naked Consumer: How Our Private Lives Become Public Commodities*. New York: Penguin, 1992.

Lebow, Victor. "Price Competition in 1955." *Journal of Retailing* 31, no. 1 (1955) 5–11.

Leclercq, Jean. *The Love of Learning and The Desire for God: A Study of Monastic Culture*. 3rd ed. New York: Fordham University Press, 1982.

Leonhardt, Megan. "Only 28% of Americans Plan to Max out Their Vacation Days This Year." *CNBC*, April 27, 2019. https://www.cnbc.com/2019/04/26/only-28percent-of-americans-plan-to-max-out-their-vacation-days-this-year.html.

Levin, Yuval. *A Time to Build: From Family and Community to Congress and the Campus, How Recommitting to Our Institutions Can Revive the American Dream*. New York: Basic, 2020.

Lewis, C. S. *Mere Christianity*. San Francisco: Harper, 2001.

———. *The Screwtape Letters*. New York: HarperOne, 2015.

———. *The Weight of Glory*. New York: HarperCollins, 2001.

Lindgren, Caleb. "State of Theology: Evangelicals Hold Steady on Doctrine, More Outspoken on Politics." *Christianity Today*. September 8, 2020. https://www.christianitytoday.com/news/2020/september/evangelicals-belief-ligonier-lifeway-theology-heresy-survey.html.

Lipka, Michael. "Religious 'Nones' Are Not Only Growing, They're Becoming More Secular." Pew Research Center, November 11, 2015. https://www.pewresearch.org/fact-tank/2015/11/11/religious-nones-are-not-only-growing-theyre-becoming-more-secular/.

Lizardo, Omar. "Improving Cultural Analysis: Considering Personal Culture in its Declarative and Nondeclarative Modes." *American Sociological Review* 82, no. 1 (2017) 88–115.

Luhrmann, T. M. *How God Becomes Real: Kindling the Presence of Invisible Others*. Princeton: Princeton University Press, 2020.

MacIntyre, Alasdair. *After Virtue: A Study in Moral Philosophy*. 2nd ed. Notre Dame: University of Notre Dame Press, 1984.

———. *God, Philosophy, Universities: A Selective History of the Catholic Philosophical Tradition*. Lanham, MA: Rowman & Littlefield, 2009.

———. *Three Rival Versions of Moral Enquiry: Encyclopaedia, Genealogy, and Tradition*. Notre Dame: University of Notre Dame Press, 1994.

MacMillan, Karl. "Pornography's Technological Handmaiden." *Humanum: Issues in Family, Culture & Science* 1 (2018). https://humanumreview.com/articles/old-friends-pornography-and-technology.

Madrigal, Alexis C. "How Much Is Your Data Worth? Mmm, Somewhere Between Half a Cent and $1,200." *The Atlantic*, March 19, 2012. https://www.theatlantic.com/technology/archive/2012/03/how-much-is-your-data-worth-mmm-somewhere-between-half-a-cent-and-1-200/254730/.

———. "How Much YouTube Do Employees Really Watch at Work?" *The Atlantic*, February 25, 2013. https://www.theatlantic.com/technology/archive/2013/02/how-much-youtube-do-employees-really-watch-at-work/273474/.

Malito, Alessandra. "Grocery Stores Carry 40,000 More Items than They Did in the 1990s." *MarketWatch*, June 17, 2017. https://www.marketwatch.com/story/grocery-stores-carry-40000-more-items-than-they-did-in-the-1990s-2017-16-07.

Bibliography

Manglos-Weber, Nicolette, and Christian Smith. *Understanding Former Young Catholics: Findings from a National Study of American Emerging Adults*. South Bend, IN: University of Notre Dame Press, 2014.

Marsden, George M. "The Soul of the American University." *First Things* (January 1991). https://www.firstthings.com/article/1991/01/the-soul-of-the-american-university.

———. *Religion and American Culture*. New York: Harcourt Brace Jovanovich, 1990.

McCabe, Mick. "McCabe: Archdiocese of Detroit Has Declared War on Athletics." *The Detroit Free Press*, May 16, 2019. https://www.freep.com/story/sports/high-school/mick-mccabe/2019/05/16/archdiocese-detroit-sunday-sports-allen-vigneron/3694394002/.

McCarty, Robert J., and John M. Vitek. *Going, Going, Gone: The Dynamics of Disaffiliation in Young Catholics*. Winona, MN: St. Mary's, 2018.

McGavran, Donald. *Understanding Church Growth*. 3rd ed. Edited by C. Peter Wagner. Grand Rapids: Eerdmans, 1990.

Miller, Alan S., and Takashi Nakamura. "On the Stability of Church Attendance Patterns during a Time of Demographic Change." *Journal for the Scientific Study of Religion* 35, no. 3 (1996) 275–84.

Miller, Vincent J. *Consuming Religion: Christian Faith and Practice in Consumer Culture*. New York: Bloomsbury Academic, 2005.

Miner, Robert C. "Aquinas on Habitus." In *A History of Habit: From Aristotle to Bourdieu*, edited by Tom Sparrow and Adam Hutchinson, 67–88. New York: Lexington, 2013.

Mishel, Lawrence, Josh Bivens, Elise Gould, and Heidi Shierholz. *The State of Working America*. 12th ed. Ithaca, NY: Cornell University Press, 2012.

Mondragon Corporation. "About Us." https://www.mondragon-corporation.com/en/about-us/.

Nasar, Jack L. "Pedestrian Injuries Due to Mobile Phone Use in Public Places." *Accident Analysis & Prevention* 57 (August 2013) 91–95.

National Catholic Educational Association. "The Catholic School Choice: Understanding the Perspectives of Parents and Opportunities for More Engagement." 2018. https://publications.fadica.org/main/Publications/tabid/101/ProdID/70/Catholic_School_Choice_Understanding_the_Perspectives_of_Parents_and_Opportunities_for_More_Engagement.aspx.

National Center for Health Statistics. "Obesity and Overweight." Centers for Disease Control and Prevention. https://www.cdc.gov/nchs/fastats/obesity-overweight.htm.

National Chicken Council. "Per Capita Consumption of Poultry and Livestock, 1960 to Forecast 2020, in Pounds." https://www.nationalchickencouncil.org/about-the-industry/statistics/per-capita-consumption-of-poultry-and-livestock-1965-to-estimated-2012-in-pounds/.

Nault, Dom Jean-Charles. *The Noonday Devil: Acedia, the Unnamed Evil of Our Times*. San Francisco: Ignatius, 2015.

Nestle, Marion, and Malden Nesheim. *Why Calories Count: From Science to Politics*. Berkeley: University of California Press, 2013.

Neuhaus, Richard John. *American Babylon: Notes of a Christian Exile*. New York: Basic Books, 2009.

The New York Times. "A Bleak Outlook Is Seen for Religion." February 25, 1968. https://www.nytimes.com/1968/02/25/archives/a-bleak-outlook-is-seen-for-religion.html.

Bibliography

Newman, John Henry. "Sermon 1. Holiness Necessary for Future Blessedness." In *Parochial and Plain Sermons*, 1–14. London: Longmans, Green, and Co, 1907. http://www.newmanreader.org/works/parochial/volume1/index.html.

———. "Sermon 5. Dispositions for Faith." In *Sermons Preached on Various Occasions*, 60–74. London: Longmans, Green, and Co, 1908.

———. *The Idea of a University*. Notre Dame: University of Notre Dame Press, 1982.

Niebuhr, H. Richard. *Christ and Culture*. New York: HarperCollins, 1951.

Nielsen. "Time Flies: U.S. Adults Now Spend Nearly Half a Day Interacting with Media." July 31, 2018. https://www.nielsen.com/us/en/insights/article/2018/time-flies-us-adults-now-spend-nearly-half-a-day-interacting-with-media/.

Nietzel, Michael T. "Whither the Humanities: The Ten-Year Trend in College Majors." *Forbes*, January 7, 2019. https://www.forbes.com/sites/michaeltnietzel/2019/01/07/whither-the-humanities-the-ten-yeari-trend-in-college-majors/?sh=5e4af7e364ad.

Nolan, James L., Jr. *What They Saw in America: Alexis de Tocqueville, Max Weber, G. K. Chesterton, and Sayyid Qutb*. New York: Cambridge University Press, 2016.

Novak, Michael. *The Spirit of Democratic Capitalism*. Lanham, MA: Madison, 1990.

Okholm, Dennis. "Staying Put to Get Somewhere." In *Christian Reflection: A Series In Faith and Ethics*, 19–25. Center for Christian Ethics at Baylor University, 2013. https://www.baylor.edu/content/services/document.php/212248.pdf.

Park, Brian, et al. "Is Internet Pornography Causing Sexual Dysfunctions? A Review with Clinical Reports." *Behavioral Sciences* 6, no. 3 (September 2016) 17.

Paul VI. *Evangelii Nuntiandi*. Apostolic exhortation. Vatican website, December 8, 1975. https://www.vatican.va/content/paul-vi/en/apost_exhortations/documents/hf_p-vi_exh_19751208_evangelii-nuntiandi.html.

Pew Research Center. "America's Changing Religious Landscape." May 12, 2015. https://www.pewforum.org/2015/05/12/americas-changing-religious-landscape/.

———. "In U.S., Decline of Christianity Continues at Rapid Pace." October 17, 2019. https://www.pewforum.org/2019/10/17/in-u-s-decline-of-christianity-continues-at-rapid-pace/.

———. "Modern Parenthood." March 14, 2013. https://www.pewsocialtrends.org/2013/03/14/modern-parenthood-roles-of-moms-and-dads-converge-as-they-balance-work-and-family/.

———. "U.S. Religious Knowledge Survey." September 28, 2010. http://www.pewforum.org/2010/09/28/u-s-religious-knowledge-survey/.

Philips, Helen. "Introduction: The Human Brain." *NewScientist*, September 4, 2006. https://www.newscientist.com/article/dn9969-introduction-the-human-brain/.

Pieper, Josef. *Leisure: The Basis of Culture*. San Francisco: Ignatius, 2009.

Pollan, Michael. "Unhappy Meals." *The New York Times Magazine*, January 28, 2007. https://michaelpollan.com/articles-archive/unhappy-meals/.

Postman, Neil. *Amusing Ourselves to Death: Public Discourse in the Age of Show Business*. New York: Penguin, 2005.

Poust, Mary DeTurris. "Pope Francis' guide to avoiding a 'throwaway culture.'" *Our Sunday Visitor*, August 21, 2013. https://osvnews.com/2013/08/21/pope-francis-guide-to-avoiding-a-throwaway-culture/.

Purdy, Chase. "After years of designing fatter birds, food companies are finally realizing chickens shouldn't grow so fast." *Quartz*, March 1, 2017. https://qz.com/922309/how-chicken-farming-works-and-why-companies-like-whole-foods-wfm-chipotle-cmg-and-tyson-foods-tsn-are-now-realizing-chickens-shouldnt-grow-so-fast/.

Bibliography

Ratzinger, Joseph. *Called to Communion: Understanding the Church Today*. San Francisco: Ignatius, 1996.
———. *Co-Workers of the Truth: Meditations for Every Day of the Year*. San Francisco: Ignatius, 1992.
———. *Images of Hope: Meditations on Major Feasts*. San Francisco: Ignatius, 2006.
———. *'In the Beginning . . .': A Catholic Understanding of the Story of Creation and the Fall*. Grand Rapids: Eerdmans, 1995.
———. "The Theological Locus of Ecclesial Movements." *Communio International Catholic Review* 25, no. 3 (1998) 480–504.
Ratzinger, Joseph, and Marcello Pera. *Without Roots: The West, Relativism, Christianity, Islam*. New York: Basic Books, 2006.
Ratzinger, Joseph, and Vittorio Messori. *The Ratzinger Report: An Exclusive Interview on the State of the Church*. San Francisco: Ignatius, 1985.
Reno, R. R. "Fighting the Noonday Devil." *First Things*, August 2003. https://www.firstthings.com/article/2003/08/fighting-the-noonday-devil.
Rieff, Phillip. *Fellow Teachers: Of Culture and Its Second Death*. Chicago: University of Chicago Press, 1985.
———. *The Triumph of the Therapeutic: Uses of Faith after Freud*. New York: Harper and Row, 1966.
Riordan, Cornelius. "Trends in student demography in Catholic secondary schools, 1972–1992." In *Catholic Schools at the Crossroads: Survival and Transformation*, edited by James Youniss and John J. Convey, 33–54. New York: Teachers College, 2000.
Rittenhouse, Bruce P. *Shopping for Meaningful Lives*. Eugene, OR: Wipf and Stock, 2013.
Ritzer, George. *The McDonaldization of Society*. 3rd ed. Thousand Oaks, CA: Pine Forge, 2000.
Rodrigues, Joshan. "Bored at Mass? A 7-Step Method to Fix That." *Aleteia*, August 12, 2017. https://aleteia.org/2017/08/12/bored-at-mass-a-7-step-method-to-fix-that/.
Rojek, Chris. *The Labour of Leisure: The Culture of Free Time*. London: Sage, 2010.
Rosen, Rebecca J. "Is This the Grossest Advertising Strategy of All Time?" *The Atlantic*, October 3, 2013. https://www.theatlantic.com/technology/archive/2013/10/is-this-the-grossest-advertising-strategy-of-all-time/280242/.
Rowland, Tracey. *Culture and the Thomist Tradition: After Vatican II*. London: Routledge, 2003.
Ryssdal, Kai. "Processed foods make up 70 percent of the U.S. diet." *Marketplace*, March 12, 2013. Podcast, 5:09. https://www.marketplace.org/2013/03/12/processed-foods-make-70-percent-us-diet/.
Safdar, Khadeeja. "Churches Target New Members, With Help From Big Data." *The Wall Street Journal*, December 26, 2021. https://www.wsj.com/articles/churches-new-members-personal-online-data-analytics-gloo-11640310982?mod=hp_lead_pos7.
Saldivia, Gabriela. "Stuck in Traffic? You're Not Alone. New Data Show American Commute Times Are Longer." *NPR*, September 20, 2018. https://www.npr.org/2018/09/20/650061560/stuck-in-traffic-youre-not-alone-new-data-show-american-commute-times-are-longer.
Sarah, Robert Cardinal. *The Power of Silence: Against the Dictatorship of Noise*. San Francisco: Ignatius, 2017.
Schatzki, Theodore R. "A Primer on Practices: Theory and Research." In *Practice-Based Education: Perspectives and Strategies*, edited by Joy Higgs, Ronald Barnett, Stephen Billet, Maggie Hutchings, and Franziska Trede, 13–26. Rotterdam: Sense, 2012.

Bibliography

Schilbrack, Kevin. "What Isn't Religion?" *The Journal of Religion* 93, no. 3 (2013) 291–318.

Schindler, D. C. *Freedom from Reality: The Diabolical Character of Modern Liberty. Catholic Ideas for a Secular World.* Notre Dame: University of Notre Dame Press, 2017.

Schindler, David L. "The Embodied Person as Gift and the Cultural Task in America: Status Quaestionis." *Communio: International Catholic Review* 35, no. 3 (2008) 397–431.

———. *Heart of the World, Center of the Church: Communio Ecclesiology, Liberalism, and Liberation.* Grand Rapids: Eerdmans, 1996.

———. *Ordering Love: Liberal Societies and the Memory of God.* Grand Rapids: Eerdmans, 2011.

———. "Toward a Culture of Life: The Eucharist, the 'Restoration' of Creation, and the 'Worldly' Task of the Laity in Liberal Societies." *Communio: International Catholic Review* 29, no. 4 (2002) 679–90.

———. "Towards a Eucharistic Evangelization." *Communio: International Catholic Review* 19, no. 4 (1992) 549–75.

———. "Trinity, Creation, and the Order of Intelligence in the Modern Academy." *Communio International Catholic Review* 28, no. 3 (2001) 407–28.

Schlosser, Eric. *Fast Food Nation: The Dark Side of The All-American Meal.* New York: Mariner, 2012.

Schor, Juliet B. *After the Gig: How the Sharing Economy Got Hijacked and How to Win It Back.* Oakland, CA: University of California Press, 2010.

———. *The Overworked American: The Unexpected Decline of Leisure.* New York: Basic Books, 1992.

Schwartz, Barry. *The Paradox of Choice: Why More Is Less.* New York: HarperCollins, 2004.

Second Vatican Council. *Lumen Gentium.* Vatican website, November 21, 1964. https://www.vatican.va/archive/hist_councils/ii_vatican_council/documents/vat-ii_const_19641121_lumen-gentium_en.html.

Sennett, Richard. *The Corrosion of Character: The Personal Consequences of Work in the New Capitalism.* New York: W. W. Norton & Company, 2000.

Smith, Adam. *Wealth of Nations.* Scotts Valley, CA: CreateSpace, 2017.

Smith, Christian, and Brandon Vaidyanathan. "Multiple Modernities and Religion." In *The Oxford Handbook of Religious Diversity*, edited by Chad V. Meister, 250–65. New York: Oxford University Press, 2011.

Smith, Christian, and Melina Lundquist Denton. *Soul Searching: The Religious and Spiritual Lives of American Teenagers.* New York: Oxford University Press, 2009.

Smith, Christian and Patricia Snell. *Souls in Transition: The Religious and Spiritual Lives of Emerging Adults.* New York: Oxford University Press, 2009.

Smith, Christian, Bridget Ritzet, and Michael Rotolo. *Religious Parenting: Transmitting Faith and Values in Contemporary America.* Princeton: Princeton University Press, 2021.

Smith, Christian, et al. *American Evangelicalism: Embattled and Thriving.* Chicago: University of Chicago Press, 1998.

Smith, Christopher C., and John Pattison. *Slow Church: Cultivating Community in the Patient Way of Jesus.* Downers Grove, IL: InterVarsity, 2014.

Smith, D. "Multitasking Undermines Our Efficiency, Study Suggests." *Monitor on Psychology* 32, no. 9 (2001) 13.

Bibliography

Smith, Gregory A. "About Three-in-Ten U.S. Adults Are Now Religiously Unaffiliated." Pew Research Center, December 14, 2021. https://www.pewforum.org/2021/12/14/about-three-in-ten-u-s-adults-are-now-religiously-unaffiliated/.

———. "Just One-Third of U.S. Catholics Agree with Their Church That Eucharist Is Body, Blood of Christ." Pew Research Center, August 5, 2019. https://www.pewresearch.org/fact-tank/2019/08/05/transubstantiation-eucharist-u-s-catholics.

Smith, James K. A. *Awaiting the King: Reforming Public Theology*. Grand Rapids: Baker Academic, 2017.

———. *Desiring the Kingdom: Worship, Worldview, and Cultural Formation*. Grand Rapids: Baker Academic, 2009.

———. *How (Not) to Be Secular: Reading Charles Taylor*. Grand Rapids: Eerdmans, 2014.

———. *Imagining the Kingdom: How Worship Works*. Grand Rapids: Baker Academic, 2013.

Smith, Jonathan Z. "Religion, Religions, Religious." In *Critical Terms for Religious Studies*, edited by Mark C. Taylor, 269–84. Chicago: University of Chicago Press, 1998.

Smith, Peter Jesserer. "Bishop Barron: How to Bring 'Nones' to Christ in a Time of Scandal." *National Catholic Register* May 30, 2019. https://www.ncregister.com/blog/pjsmith/bishop-barron-how-to-bring-nones-to-christ-in-a-time-of-scandal.

Staff reports. "Southern Baptist Convention Continues Statistical Decline, Floyd Calls for Rethinking ACP Process." *Baptist Press*, June 4, 2020. https://www.baptistpress.com/resource-library/news/southern-baptist-convention-continues-statistical-decline-floyd-calls-for-rethinking-acp-process/.

Stark, Rodney, and Roger Finke. *Acts of Faith: Explaining the Human Side of Religion*. Berkeley: University of California Press, 2000.

Stober, Clare. *Another Life Is Possible: Insights from 100 Years of Life Together*. Walden, NY: Plough, 2020.

Stolzenberg, Ross M., et al. "Religious Participation in Early Adulthood: Age and Family Life Cycle Effects on Church Membership." *American Sociological Review* 60, no. 1 (1995) 84–103.

Swidler, Ann. *Talk of Love: How Culture Matters*. Chicago: University of Chicago Press, 2001.

SWNS. "Americans Check Their Phones 80 Times a Day: Study." *New York Post,* November 8, 2017. https://nypost.com/2017/11/08/americans-check-their-phones-80-times-a-day-study/.

Taylor, Charles. *A Secular Age*. Cambridge: Belknap Press of Harvard University Press, 2018.

———. *Modern Social Imaginaries*. Durham, NC: Duke University Press, 2004.

Teresa of Avila. *The Collected Works of Saint Teresa of Avila*. Vol. 1. Translated by Kieran Kavanaugh and Otilio Rodriguez. Washington, DC: ICS Publications, 1987.

Thorton, Patricia H., and William Ocasio. "Institutional Logics." In *The SAGE Handbook of Organizational Institutionalism,* edited by Royston Greenwood, Christine Oliver, Roy Suddaby, and Kerstin Sahlin, 99–129. London: SAGE, 2008.

Tradistae. "'A New Set of Social Forms': Alasdair MacIntyre on the 'Benedict Option.'" Blog post, April 21, 2020. https://tradistae.com/2020/04/21/macintyre-benop/.

Tramontin, Kelly. "Instagram as an Evangelizing Tool." *Word on Fire Blog,* November 6, 2019. https://www.wordonfire.org/resources/blog/instagram-as-an-evangelizing-tool/25758/.

Bibliography

Tschannen, Olivier. "The Secularization Paradigm: A Systematization." *Journal for the Scientific Study of Religion* 30, no. 4 (1991) 395–415.

Twitchell, James. *Shopping for God: How Christianity Went from in Your Heart to in Your Face.* New York: Simon & Schuster, 2007.

U.S. Census Bureau. "Median and Average Square Feet of Floor Plan Area in New Single-Family Houses Completed by Location." https://www.census.gov/const/C25Ann/sftotalmedavgsqft.pdf.

Uecker, Jeremy E. "Alternative Schooling Strategies and the Religious Lives of American Adolescents." *Journal for the Scientific Study of Religion* 47, no. 4. (2008) 563–84.

———. "Catholic Schooling, Protestant Schooling, and Religious Commitment in Young Adulthood." *Journal for the Scientific Study of Religion* 48, no. 2 (2009) 353–67.

Vaidyanathan, Brandon. "Religious Resources or Differential Returns? Early Religious Socialization and Declining Attendance in Emerging Adulthood." *Journal for the Scientific Study of Religion* 50, no. 2 (2011) 366–87.

Vaisey, Stephen. "Motivation and Justification: A Dual-Process Model of Culture in Action." *American Journal of Sociology* 114, no. 6 (2009) 1675–1715.

———. "Socrates, Skinner, and Aristotle: Three Ways of Thinking About Culture in Action." *Sociological Forum* 23, no. 3 (2008) 603–13.

Wager, Emma, et al. "How does health spending in the U.S. compare to other countries?" *Health System Tracker,* January 21, 2022. https://www.healthsystemtracker.org/chart-collection/health-spending-u-s-compare-countries-2/#item-spendingcomparison_health-consumption-expenditures-per-capita-2019.

Wang, Y., and, M. A. Beydoun. "Meat Consumption Is Associated with Obesity and Central Obesity Among US Adults." *International Journal of Obesity* 33 (2009) 621–28.

Weber, Jeremy. "Christian, What Do You Believe? Probably a Heresy About Jesus, Says Survey." *Christianity Today,* October 16, 2018. https://www.christianitytoday.com/news/2018/october/what-do-christians-believe-ligonier-state-theology-heresy.html.

Weber, Max. *The Protestant Ethic and the Spirit of Capitalism.* New York: Routledge, 2001.

WebFX. "What Are Data Brokers—And What Is Your Data Worth?" March 16, 2020. https://www.webfx.com/blog/internet/what-are-data-brokers-and-what-is-your-data-worth-infographic/.

Weinfuss, Josh. "Kingsbury to allow Cardinals 'cellphone breaks.'" *ESPN.com,* March 26, 2019. https://www.espn.com/nfl/story/_/id/26368658/kingsbury-allow-cardinals-cellphone-breaks.

White, Michael, and Tom Corcoran. *Rebuilt: Awakening the Faithful, Reaching the Lost, and Making Church Matter.* Notre Dame: Ave Maria, 2013.

Wilde, Oscar. *The Picture of Dorien Gray.* The Project Gutenberg. Ebook, 2008. https://www.gutenberg.org/files/26740/26740-h/26740-h.htm.

Willard, Dallas. *The Spirit of the Disciplines: Understanding How God Changes Lives.* New York: HarperCollins, 1999.

Williams, Raymond. *Keywords: A Vocabulary of Culture and Society.* New ed. New York: Oxford University Press, 2015.

Wilson, James Matthew. "The Law of Art." *The Catholic Thing,* November 13, 2019. https://www.thecatholicthing.org/2019/11/13/the-law-of-art/.

Wilson, Timothy. *Strangers to Ourselves: Discovering the Adaptive Unconscious.* Cambridge: Belknap Press of Harvard University Press, 2002.

Wirzba, Norman. *Food and Faith: A Theology of Eating*. Cambridge: Cambridge University Press, 2007.

———. *Living the Sabbath: Discovering the Rhythms of Rest and Delight*. Grand Rapids: Brazos, 2006.

Wojtyla, Karol. *Person and Community: Selected Essays*. Translated by Theresa H. Sandok. New York: Peter Lang, 1993.

Woods, Robert M. "Religion: The Key to Christopher Dawson's Culture." *The Imaginative Conservative*. https://theimaginativeconservative.org/2015/05/religion-the-key-to-christopher-dawsons-culture.html.

Wuthnow, Robert. *God and Mammon in America*. New York: Free Press, 1994.

———. "In Polling We Trust." *First Things* (August/September 2015) 39–44.

———. *Poor Richard's Principle*. Princeton: Princeton University Press, 1998.

Yamane, David. *Becoming Catholic: Finding Rome in the American Religious Landscape*. New York: Oxford University Press, 2014.

Index

acedia, 73–76, 86–87
advertising, 52–54, 63–64
alienation, 42–45, 59–60
Alpha, 100–101
anti-eucharistic society, 57–62
Aquinas, Saint Thomas, 12, 73, 86–87
    definition of religion, 8–9
Augustine, Saint, 8, 15

Barron, Bishop Robert, 95, 98
beliefs,
    importance of, xv
Benedict Option. *See* Dreher, Rod.
Berger, Peter, 3
Bruderhof, 118–19
busyness, 45–46

Catholic schools, 32–33, 45, 117–18
Cavanaugh, William, 107, 112n16
choice, 54–56
Church Growth Movement, 91–95
commodification, 38–42
conversion, 98–99, 102–3
creation, 14–15, 22, 31, 83
cultural liturgies, xv–xvi
Culture of Death, 16–18, 27–28, 45, 47
culture, xiii–xv, xvii, 1–2, 11–13

De Tocqueville, Alexis, 38
Deneen, Patrick, 123
disenchantment, 3, 6n31
dispositions, xviii, 9–14, 18–19, 24, 79–80, 111
Dostoevsky, Fyodor, 120
Dreher, Rod, 114–15, 123

evangelization, 95–99

freedom, 22, 46, 55, 64–65
    religious, 62–65

Galbraith, John Kenneth, 51–52

Hauerwas, Stanley, 108
Hunter, James Davison, 110–11

intentional community, 114–19

John Paul II. *See* Pope John Paul II.

Kreeft, Peter, 94

leisure, 66–68
    labor of, 67–68, 77
Lewis, C.S., xvi, 50, 74, 86–87
liberal arts, 33–34

Index

MacIntyre, Alasdair, 13n62, 21, 119n30, 122–23
martyrdom, 111–13
McDonaldization, 36–37, 90
Ministry-Industrial Complex, 100–103
Mondragon Corporation, 116

Newman, John Henry, 76
nones, 95
novelty, 70–72

O'Connor, Flannery, 105

Pascal, Blaise, 72
Polanyi, Michael, 12
politics, 107–9
Pope Benedict XVI, 31, 104, 112, 123
Pope Francis, 57
Pope John Paul II, xvii-xviii, 16–18, 27–28, 35, 37–42, 45–46, 55, 64–65, 81–82, 89, 99
PowerPoint, 24, 31
practical atheism, xviii, 18–19, 80–88
practices, xv-xvii, 10–14

Ratzinger, Joseph. See Pope Benedict XVI
RCIA, 103
religion, definition of, 6–7

sabbath, 66–67, 77–78
Schindler, David L., 14–15, 29n23, 48–49, 123
Second Vatican Council, xi, xiii-xiv, 48n63
secularization theory, 2–6
Smith, Adam, 48
Smith, Christian, 26
Smith, James K. A., 13, 19, 89
social media, 95–99

Taylor, Charles, 5–10, 93
theological ignorance, xii

Vatican II. *See* Second Vatican Council.
virtue, xvi, 12
  religion as, 6–14
  counterfeit, 83–85

Weber, Max, 38, 43n48, 89–90